AFRICA'S
NEW LEADERS
DEMOCRACY OR STATE
RECONSTRUCTION?

MARINA OTTAWAY

D1042530

CARNEGIE ENDOWMENT FOR INTERNATIONAL PEACE

Africa's New Leaders:
Democracy or State Reconstruction?
may be ordered (**$10.95** paper) from Carnegie's distributor:
The Brookings Institution Press
Department 029, Washington, D.C. 20042-0029, USA
Tel: 1-800-275-1447 or 202-797-6258
Fax: 202-797-6004
E-mail: bibooks@brook.edu

Library of Congress Cataloging-in-Publication Data

Ottaway, Marina
    Africa's new leaders: democracy or state reconstruction? / Marina
    Ottaway.
           p.   cm.
    "A Carnegie Endowment book."
    Includes bibliographical references.
    ISBN 0-87003-134-1
    1. Africa, Eastern—Politics and government—1960- 2. Democracy—
Africa, Eastern—History—20th century. 3. Monarch—Africa, Eastern—
History—20th century. I. Title. II. Title: Africa's new leaders.
DT365.78.088   1999   98-55067
320.963'09'049—dc2   CIP

Edited by Valeriana Kallab.
Design by Paddy McLaughlin Concepts & Design.
Cover Photo: Jose Azel/Aurora/PNI.
Printed by Automated Graphic Systems, Inc.

CONTENTS

FOREWORD   v

1. INTRODUCTION   1
    Promoting Democracy in Africa   5
    Understanding the Policies   9
    Democratic Transitions in Africa   11
    Focus and Objectives of this Study   13

2. THE BACKGROUND   15
    Ethiopia and Eritrea   15
    Uganda   19
    The Challenge of Rebuilding the State   22
    What Kind of Transition?   26

3. UGANDA AND THE POLITICS OF PROCESS   29
    Rebuilding the State   32
    Increasing Participation   39
    Conclusions   45

4. ERITREA: COMMAND STATE AND MARKET ECONOMY   47
    Building the New State   48
    The Issue of Participation   58
    Conclusions   62

5. ETHIOPIA AND THE CHALLENGE
OF POLITICIZED ETHNICITY   65
    Rebuilding the State   66
    The Issue of Democracy   77
    Conclusions   81

6. FOLLOWING THE EXAMPLE? RWANDA AND
THE DEMOCRATIC REPUBLIC OF THE CONGO   83
    Rwanda   84
    The Democratic Republic of the Congo   92
    Conclusions   100

7. GOING BEYOND THE BORDERS   **101**
The Failure of International Institutions   102
The Chain of Crises   106
Policies Without Rules   109
African Solutions for African Problems   115

8. LOOKING AHEAD   **117**
Commonalities: Transformation from the Top
and the Creation of Political Space   118
Differences: Political Strategies and
the Logic of Economic Transformation   120
Problems of Transition   122
Promoting Democracy: The Long View   130

About the Author   135
About the Carnegie Endowment   137

FOREWORD

The 1990s opened with great optimism for the global spread of democracy. Samuel Huntington had not even finished writing his account of the 1970s–1980s "third wave" when the collapse of communism set off a frenzied round of regime transformations, this time in Central and Eastern Europe and the states of what would soon become the former Soviet Union. The end of the Cold War raised hopes that political democracies and market economies might evolve from post-colonial authoritarian regimes in Africa as well, particularly if they were prodded by Western financial aid and newly designed democracy assistance programs.

As the decade draws to a close, this early optimism has faded. Despite some notable successes, the spread of democracy in the past decade has not been as rapid or problem-free as some predicted and many had hoped. In Africa, a small number of states have made progress toward genuine multi-party elections and peaceable transitions. A much larger number, however, superficially adhere to democratic norms without democratic substance—or remain unreconstructed authoritarian regimes with no pretense of democracy. In addition to Africa's long-standing problems of poverty and underdevelopment, the continent in recent years has suffered horrific genocides, ongoing massacres of civilians, and a series of coups d'état and civil wars that now threaten to draw neighboring states into regional conflicts they can ill afford to fight.

For most of the 1990s, promoting the spread of democracy has been an explicit goal of U.S. diplomacy. With the relatively easy transitions, mostly in Central Europe, now apparently behind us, the future of democracy promotion will involve the tougher cases that observers label "illiberal," "stagnating," or "virtual" democracies, for which the current policies of the United States and other countries have proven inadequate or misguided. In designing better approaches, policy makers will need not only grand theory, but deep understanding of individual countries—precisely the kind of detail and insight Marina Ottaway offers in *Africa's New Leaders: Democracy or State Reconstruction?*

Presidents Yoweri Museveni of Uganda and Isaias Afwerki of Eritrea and Prime Minister Meles Zenawi of Ethiopia deserve to be called "new leaders," Ottaway suggests, not because of chronological age but because of their new approaches to governing. Unlike older-style African rulers who tyrannized their subjects while expropriating their wealth, these new statesmen appear genuinely committed to improving the lives of their countrymen. But in choosing to concentrate on state reconstruction over the immediate introduction of competitive multi-party elections and a free press, the new leaders defy the donors' prescription for democratic change. And their aggressive foreign policies in nearby states such as Rwanda, the Democratic Republic of the Congo, and the Sudan often put them at odds with the international community.

Models of democratic transition that assume stable states and pluralistic societies are too simplistic for much of Africa, Ottaway argues. The problem of African states is not only the absence of democratic institutions for participation, but also the weakness of the basic administrative apparatus necessary to maintain security, administer the territory, and implement policy decisions. In the pages that follow, Ottaway begins what should become a serious international debate on how best to promote democracy in countries where the state itself is in need of reconstruction.

Marina Ottaway is a Senior Associate and Co-Director of the Democracy and Rule of Law Project at the Carnegie Endowment for International Peace. Her work on this publication was supported by a grant from the Ford Foundation, whose support is gratefully acknowledged.

Jessica T. Mathews
President

February 1999
Washington, D.C.

AFRICA'S NEW LEADERS

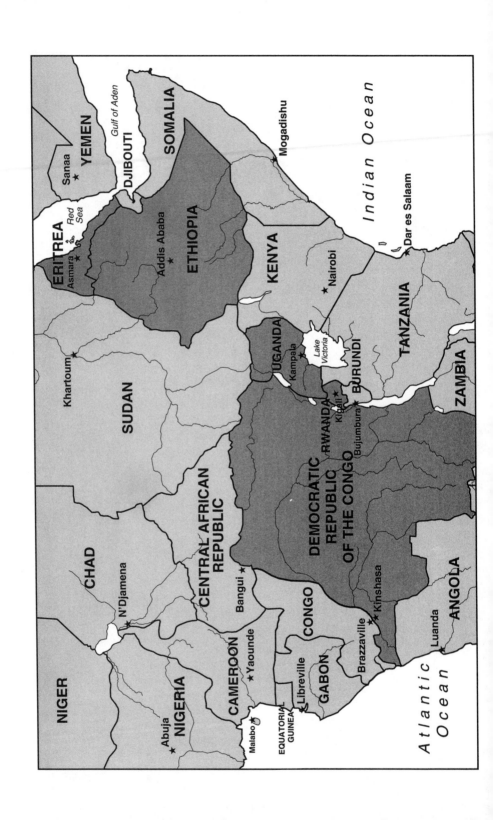

INTRODUCTION

This study starts from the obvious assumption that what is most desirable is not necessarily possible. The quick transformation of highly authoritarian countries into democratic ones is very desirable. In most cases, it is not possible. The job of policy makers is to figure out the difference between the desirable and the possible and to tailor decisions accordingly. This study seeks to help distinguish between the desirable and the possible in the area of democracy promotion, using the example of three African countries: Uganda, Eritrea, and Ethiopia.

These three countries, and to a lesser extent Rwanda, have attracted a great deal of attention, both negative and positive, since the mid-1990s. Under the leadership of dynamic, assertive leaders, the countries have started to stabilize after prolonged periods of conflict. Their mechanisms of government and administration have slowly been re-established. Their economies have experienced healthy growth rates. To be sure, all three countries remain very poor, and all contain substantial pockets of conflict and instability. Nevertheless, the change has been such that the more optimistic observers see these countries as forerunners of an African renaissance. They also perceive their leaders—President Yoweri Museveni of Uganda, President Isaias Afwerki of Eritrea, and Prime Minister Meles Zenawi of Ethiopia—as the best representatives of Africa's "new leaders" and the epitome of a new generation of statesmen who have rejected the failed policies of their predecessors and are ready to take on the challenges of the global economy and the post–Cold War world.

The achievements of the new leaders, at least relative to conditions in most African countries, have attracted the attention of donors anxious to contribute to some African success stories rather than see their aid disappear without trace in the quagmire of poorly managed and led countries. Bilateral donors and international financial institutions alike have made a substantial commitment to the three countries. In the case of the United States, security concerns have further strengthened the relationship. Uganda, Ethiopia, and Eritrea border the Sudan. Controlled by an Islamist government willing to harbor extremist organizations, the Sudan is considered a terrorist country. Containing the Sudan is thus a goal of U.S. policy. The three countries, which have their own reasons to fear and to oppose the Sudanese regime, are seen as natural allies in this containment policy.

As leaders of countries that allow the United States to smoothly combine its own security considerations with support for a promising new trend in Africa, Museveni, Meles, and Isaias have been lionized.[1] When Madeleine Albright visited Africa in December 1997—in a rare trip to that continent by an American secretary of state—she made a point of going to Uganda and Ethiopia, where she spoke glowingly of the emerging partnership between the United States and these countries. During an even rarer visit by an American president, President Clinton in April 1998 stopped in Uganda, where he also convoked Isaias and Meles together with other heads of state in the region; on the same trip, the president also visited Rwanda. Clearly the new leaders figure prominently in U.S. policy toward Africa.

But there is another side to these countries, and as soon as Albright's and Clinton's visits opened them to greater scrutiny, doubts began to be voiced about the wisdom of the emerging close relationship. Uganda, Ethiopia, and Eritrea are not democratic countries, despite the rhetoric of U.S. officials during their visits; indeed, the new leaders argue vehemently and at times eloquently against the adoption of competitive, multi-party democracy in the near future. Any attempt to introduce such a system suddenly, they claim, would just plunge their countries back into chaos, undoing what has been achieved in terms of economic reconstruction and long-term political change. Furthermore, these countries pursue aggressive foreign policies, often in defiance of fundamental principles of international rela-

---

[1] Ethiopians and Eritreans have a first name and a patronymic, but no last name. The two heads of state are thus correctly addressed as Meles and Isaias, not Zenawi and Afwerki, who are their respective fathers.

tions.. Their leaders like to think of themselves as statesmen capable of providing the solutions to regional conflicts that have eluded the efforts of the international community, but their policies are creating new conflicts. After falling out with each other in mid-1998 in a border dispute, Eritrea and Ethiopia remain close to war, and the interventions by Rwanda and Uganda in Zaire in 1996-97 and again in 1998 (by which time the country was known as the Democratic Republic of the Congo) have increased rather than diminished the turmoil in the entire region. The critics of the Clinton Administration's Africa policy maintain that the United States is not supporting a new generation of leaders and an African renaissance, but that it has simply fallen back into Cold War–vintage policies of supporting governments with questionable credentials whenever it suits U.S. security needs.

Underlying these conflicting interpretations of the new leaders are different assumptions about what is possible during a country's transition from civil war and authoritarianism— whether it can move directly toward democracy, or whether the problems it faces make it imperative that it tackle other issues first. The detractors of the three regimes believe that a democratic transition is always possible, no matter what the initial conditions, and that multi-party elections are the starting point. They thus dismiss the new leaders' views on democracy as a self-serving rationale that masks a basic authoritarian intent. Those who judge the three regimes in a positive light are skeptical about the possibility of quick democratic transformations in all countries. The new leaders' assertions about the dangers of democracy are plausible enough, given the prevailing conditions, to give pause. It is not that a fully democratic system would not be desirable. The problem is getting from here to there: the path of transformation prescribed by aid donors ignores conditions and fails to address many urgent problems. Uganda, Ethiopia, and Eritrea are at least addressing many such problems successfully and must be given the benefit of the doubt that their approach will, as they claim, eventually lead to democracy.

The contradiction between what is desirable in terms of goals and what is possible in terms of process makes these countries a test of the capacity of the United States and other donors to remain true to the stated goals of democracy promotion with-

3

out being unrealistic about how transformation can take place. The United States faces similar challenges in other (and, indeed, politically more important) countries. What makes these three particularly interesting is that the choice between what is desirable in theory and what is possible in practice need not be overshadowed by other considerations. In the case of China, for example, commitment to democratization conflicts directly with U.S. economic and security interests. But Uganda, Eritrea, and Ethiopia are no Chinas. Their economic importance to the United States is nonexistent, and their security importance is marginal at best—they all share a border with the Sudan, considered by the United States to be a terrorist state, but can do little to help the United States fight international terrorism. Thus it would be conceivable for the United States to pursue a policy toward Uganda, Eritrea, and Ethiopia that is based purely on principles, as many non-governmental organizations (NGOs) want, sending a clear signal that the United States cares about democracy. This makes the present policy of engagement particularly controversial.

Given the lack of direct U.S. interests in the three countries, their experience raises particularly clearly the essential question of how a democratic transformation unfolds and how it can be encouraged. Are the changes taking place in these countries stepping-stones in a long-term process of democratization—one that is unorthodox but nevertheless effective? Or are they early indications of the re-consolidation of authoritarian systems? The questions are difficult to answer because, in reality, we know little about democratization. Historical studies of democratic transformations in specific countries trace enormously complicated, conflictual, socio-economic and political processes stretching over many decades, if not centuries. While such studies should be required reading for practitioners of democratic assistance as an antidote to complacency, they do not offer much help in formulating policy. Prescriptions for democratization by international donors go to the opposite extreme, envisaging a sequence of stereotyped steps that appear ludicrously simplistic when compared with the historical record. The road to democracy is seen as a linear path any country can enter as long as the will is there. The path starts with a short period of liberalization, followed by a democratic transition achieved through the holding of multi-party elections, and winds on to its final destination through a long stretch of democratic consolidation. Countries are pressed to approach democratization by focusing on mechanisms: amend the constitution, write laws on political parties, form electoral commissions, carry out civic education, hold multi-party elections. Little attention is paid to the fundamental question of whether these mechanisms address the real problems the countries face. This study will attempt to steer a middle course, going beyond the question of whether the three countries are following the currently prescribed process of transformation—the answer is a clear but unhelpful "no"—but avoiding broad historical analysis. It will describe instead how these countries are changing and seek to explain the rationale that guides their policies and the imperatives that their governments must address just to survive and avoid the disintegration of the state. Donor attempts to promote democracy are likely to be futile unless they also address such imperatives.

The study does not claim that the policies followed by the three countries represent a successful model of democratic transformation in African countries or, more broadly, in countries emerging from civil war. On the contrary, these policies address some serious problems, but they are also causing new ones to appear. Nevertheless, the experience of the three countries calls attention to the vast array of problems that the international community fails to address in its approach to democratization. It also suggests that donors need to rethink their own approaches if their advice is to remain relevant to the process of change under way in these countries and in the many others that are caught between the authoritarianism of the Cold War era, which most have rejected, and a West-imposed path to democracy, which bears little relation to the problems they face.

PROMOTING DEMOCRACY IN AFRICA

Since the majority of African countries became independent in the early 1960s, the African political landscape has been affected by successive waves of political ideals. In the 1960s and early 1970s, African socialism dominated the African political consciousness. Then came Marxism-Leninism. During the 1990s, it was the turn of democracy, as popular discontent with plummeting living standards and the corruption and incompetence of existing regimes increased pressure for more accountable government.

In each period, only a minority of regimes conformed to the dominant model, and even those that did achieved scant results. Through the successive phases, most African countries remained mired in a loosely administered, pre-bureaucratic authoritarianism under civilian or military rulers that became widely known as "neo-patrimonialism." Nevertheless, the dominant ideal did impart a special character to each period, providing the identity for many regimes and, most important, the language through which they sought to legitimize themselves.

Having watched the growth of African socialism with skepticism and that of Marxism-Leninism with hostility, the United States and other industrialized countries have welcomed the apparent ascendance of democratic ideals during the 1990s with enthusiasm. Africa finally appears to be coming of age, abandoning the radicalism and the claim to uniqueness common in the early post-independence period, and accepting instead the universal validity of democracy and the political reality of the post–Cold War period. Donor countries, for the first time ideologically in tune with Africa, have launched an array of programs to support democratic transformation. The establishment and consolidation of democratic regimes has become one of the major goals of U.S. policy toward African countries. Other donors also stress democracy. Even the international financial institutions, which do not concern themselves directly with political change, indirectly promote more accountable and responsible government with their stress on good governance.

Domestic pressure, coupled with foreign carrots and sticks, has brought about some remarkable changes. Political language in Africa in the 1990s has become virtually unrecognizable to those familiar with the rhetoric of the 1960s–1980s: at the center of the discourse are no longer the downtrodden popular masses in whose name governments long justified authoritarian rule, but the right of an organized civil society to demand transparency and accountability from the government. Political systems are beginning to look different from the single-party model that dominated Africa for decades. Most African countries have made at least a formal transition to multi-party rule and competitive elections—although with different degrees of fairness and openness. Some die-hard authoritarian regimes refuse to accept the message that the old political ways of post-independence Africa are no longer acceptable, but their number is not large.

Democracy assistance is not the cause of this change. Underpinning the transformation is the failure of most African governments to develop viable political systems and the mounting discontent of ordinary citizens with their living conditions. Stagnant during the 1970s, most countries experienced a sharp decline in gross domestic product (GDP) during the 1980s; this translated directly into fewer jobs, more expensive food, and the decay of education and health systems. The sudden collapse of the socialist regimes in Europe demonstrated that even authoritarian governments controlling much stronger bureaucracies and repressive apparatuses than Africa's are vulnerable to popular pressure. In some countries, broad-based coalitions have formed to challenge the incumbents. More often, elites and small groups have spearheaded the process of change. The emergence of a cohesive opposition has been the crucial factor in the change. Where opposition leaders have remained divided, as in Kenya, or have allowed themselves to be co-opted, as in Zaire, neither popular discontent nor the carrots and sticks of foreign donors have succeeded in bringing about change.

It is democracy assistance, however, that has provided the new political language of "transparency" and "accountability," codified the process through which democratization is to be attained, and influenced the form of the emerging institutions. Foreign assistance thus has given democratic transformation a certain stereotyped character. It made possible, at times even imposed, the holding of elections very early in the process of transformation, even in countries where the opposition is weakly organized or civil strife impedes freedom of movement. Democracy assistance has also sought to put an imprint on constitutions and parliaments and on judiciary and legal systems, and it has made "civil society" synonymous with a narrow range of human rights and civic education institutions favored by donors. Foreign donors have not brought political change to Africa, in other words, but they have tried to shape the process and the outcome to a remarkable extent.

Have these changes and these efforts made Africa more democratic? Opinions differ widely.[2] The forms and language of government have changed almost everywhere; the content, not surprisingly, shows many traits from the past, with elected governments displaying illiberal tendencies and leaders refusing to step down when the time comes and seeking re-election in defiance of constitutional term limits. Furthermore, the wave of democratization in Africa appears to have crested, and a reflux is becoming evident. The specter of military intervention is reviving: the military deposed elected leaders in Burundi in 1993, in Gambia in 1994, in Niger in 1996, and in Sierra Leone and the Congo (Brazzaville) in 1997. In Nigeria, the military has refused to accept the outcome of the 1993 elections and has remained in power; only the death of General Sani Abacha in June 1998 has reopened the possibility of a return to civilian rule. In Ghana, a military regime has been legitimized through two successive elections, but it is still an open question to what extent Jerry Rawlings's power is rooted in his control of the military rather than in his election victory. In other countries, for example in Zambia, it is the elected regimes that show unmistakable symptoms of an authoritarian reversal. And in many countries where the forms of democracy are respected, the voters' choice is creating dominant-party systems, where one party can be expected to remain unchallenged for a long time; South Africa is the most important example. Democratic transitions are turning out to be much more complex processes, with a much more uncertain outcome, than was admitted in the initial period of euphoria.

The problem is not limited to Africa. In a growing number of countries around the world, particularly among those with the lowest levels of economic development and the weakest democratic traditions, the limits of the model of transition to democracy favored by the United States are becoming evident. Many countries have gone through the motions of democracy without developing the content. These are the "illiberal democracies" denounced by Fareed Zakaria, and the countries that led Robert Kaplan to conclude that democracy was just a moment.[3] While

---

[2] See, for example, the series of articles on "African Ambiguities" in *Journal of Democracy*, Vol. 9, 2, April 1998, pp. 1-75.

[3] Fareed Zakaria, "The Rise of Illiberal Democracy," *Foreign Affairs*, November/ December 1997, pp. 22-43; and Robert D. Kaplan, "Was Democracy Just a Moment?" *Atlantic Monthly*, December 1997, pp. 55-80.

such articles might be unduly pessimistic and above all hasty in their conclusions, they point to an undeniable fact: countries that hurry through the formal paces of a democratic transformation do not necessarily get there any faster than countries that follow a less direct path.

The fact that the dominant model of democratization has led to rather uncertain results in Africa provides an additional reason to explore the experience of Uganda, Eritrea, and Ethiopia. Their approach to transformation is, as we shall see, problematic, but no more so than the one prescribed by the donors. Something can be learned from it.

UNDERSTANDING THE POLICIES

The political transformation taking place in Uganda, Ethiopia, and Eritrea owes very little to donor pressure and assistance. Rather, it has been driven almost completely by urgent internal problems. The economic transformation of the three countries has been influenced to a much larger extent by the dominant ideas concerning the necessity of economic liberalization. Ethiopia and Eritrea, however, have also clung determinedly to some policies that they consider to be necessary for their countries' progress, even though these go against the "Washington consensus"—the free-market principles upheld by the international financial institutions.

The policies pursued by the three countries are not identical. They do, however, share a common logic antithetical to that of the donors. The new leaders have started by dealing with the problems they confront now, with much less concern for the final outcome. Indeed, Museveni, Isaias, and Meles have all stated in one form or another that, if their present policies are successful, they will have to be modified radically in the future. The donors, in contrast, are approaching the problem of political transformation in African countries with a ready-made solution: democracy must be the outcome, and it is assumed that policies designed to promote democracy will solve all other problems as well.

The next chapter of this study will seek to identify more systematically the problems that the three countries face and the logic of the policies they are following. Here, it may be useful to

9

highlight briefly the common characteristics of these policies and the questions they raise about the validity of the donors' efforts to promote democracy.

The background shared by the three countries is one of protracted turmoil. All three governments initially faced the urgent task of stabilizing the country after a devastating civil war and reconstructing a state greatly weakened by conflict—or, in Eritrea, building a new state emerging from conflict. These problems have determined the policies of the three governments. First, the governments have all devoted much effort to strengthening the administrative system. Second, they have made a strong commitment to economic reform to move from statist to market systems. They have instituted successful stabilization programs, made a commitment to economic liberalization, and achieved healthy growth rates. As a result, they have enjoyed generally good relations with the international financial institutions, and they have been able to win at least grudging acceptance of their less orthodox policies. Given the fact that the top officials of all three countries, including Museveni, Isaias, and Meles, started their political careers as socialists, it is even more remarkable that they are now seen as some of the African leaders most committed to structural adjustment. Finally, all three governments have tried to broaden their political bases and to acquire a popular mandate of sorts—not by exposing themselves to unfettered political competition, but by relying on a mixture of direct popular participation in local councils and co-optation of officials from other political organizations. But this participation falls far short of democracy.

In these attempts at transformation, leaders have played a much more important role than institutions. Museveni, Isaias, and Meles are dominant figures, and they put a strong imprint on the policies. They have been extremely outspoken and have not hesitated to denounce the hypocrisy of the donors, the self-righteousness of international NGOs, or the failures of international institutions. They have pursued assertive foreign policies in the region and have showed little respect for the most sacred principle of African foreign policy: non-interference in the affairs of other sovereign states. When they have confronted problems originating outside their borders, they have sought solutions outside their borders, as they did when they contributed to the overthrow of President Mobutu Sese Seko in Zaire. Strong leadership has been key to the success of the three countries; it has imparted a sense of direction in the absence of established institutions that more democratic and inevitably weaker executives could not have provided. But strong leadership is also extremely dangerous. Museveni, Isaias, and Meles have been innovative leaders capable of charting a new course for their countries, but only a tenuous line divides them from the "big men" of the early post-independence period, who coasted along on the initial success, never learned when it was time to quit, and failed to build durable institutions.

DEMOCRATIC TRANSITIONS IN AFRICA

The policies of the new leaders center on the reconstruction of the state and the economy—in other words, on stability and growth. By contrast, democracy is considered premature and receives scant attention. Donors, on the other hand, place the emphasis on democracy and economic reconstruction but take the state for granted. The experiences of Uganda, Ethiopia, and Eritrea—while recently more positive than those of most African countries—inevitably reopen the old debate about whether democracy addresses the problems of African countries.

As pointed out earlier, the path to democracy is complex and little understood. We do know, however, that democratic systems are more prevalent in countries where certain conditions obtain, and Africa is at a disadvantage in all of them. An obvious but often forgotten point is that democracy is a political system that presupposes the existence of the state. The state—as a de facto, functioning entity with a government that actually governs, rather than as a de jure quasi-state that owes its existence above all to international recognition—cannot be taken for granted in Africa.[4] Least of all can it be taken for granted in countries emerging from protracted conflict.

Other indicators usually associated with democracy are also unfavorable in Africa. Per capita income in most African countries is well below the threshold that appears to guarantee the

---

4 Robert Jackson, *Quasi-States: Sovereignty, International Relations, and the Third World* (Cambridge: Cambridge University Press, 1990).

11

survival of democratic regimes.[5] Economic systems, class structures, and levels of educational achievement are not those found to favor democratic transitions.[6] African political traditions and organizational structures also contribute to the pessimistic prognosis.[7] As a result, the transition process is likely to be slower, more difficult, and above all less direct than was envisaged in the early 1990s when, in the post–Cold War euphoria, the return of multi-party elections and the ouster by the electorate of some well-entrenched leaders were interpreted as signs of a democratic rebirth.

African countries undoubtedly need political change, and African citizens have made it clear in a variety of ways that they want change. But change does not necessarily mean democracy. Despite its politically incorrect antecedents, the question must be asked anew whether all countries can be assumed to be ready for democracy. The issue is not whether all people have the ability to make informed choices, but whether they have access to even minimal information; not whether poor people are mired in non-democratic traditions, but whether the weakness of the economy prevents opposition political parties, independent media, and professional NGOs from finding sufficient financial support to be effective. Thus the questions must focus on *conditions*, not on the personal attributes of the citizens.

The policies pursued by Uganda, Ethiopia, and Eritrea are a good reminder of what is still missing in many African countries—ranging from the state's capacity to maintain minimal security, to the bureaucracy's ability to implement policy, to sufficient economic activity to keep people alive, let alone provide the funds to support political organizations and NGOs. Trying to solve such basic problems is not democracy, but progress toward democracy is unlikely unless such problems are solved to some degree.

---

[5] See Adam Przeworski, *Democracy and the Market* (Cambridge: Cambridge University Press, 1991); and Samuel P. Huntington, *The Third Wave* (Norman, Okla.: University of Oklahoma Press, 1991).

[6] See Seymour Martin Lipset, "Some Social Requisites for Democracy, Economic Development and Political Legitimacy," *American Political Science Review*, Vol. 53, 1, pp. 69-105; and Barrington Moore, *The Social Origins of Dictatorship and Democracy* (Boston: Beacon Press, 1967).

[7] See Michael Bratton and Nicolas Van de Walle, *Democratic Experiments in Africa* (Cambridge: Cambridge University Press, 1997); Samuel P. Huntington, "The Clash of Civilizations," *Foreign Affairs*, Summer 1993.

The challenge that Uganda, Ethiopia, and Eritrea pose for the donors is that of distinguishing between those policies which deviate from the democratization model suggested by the donors because the model does not address the urgent problems the countries face, and those policies which deviate from the model because the country is slipping back toward authoritarianism. A better understanding of the countries—the goals of the leaders, the policies they are following, their intentions as well as the outcomes—is the first step toward making that distinction and answering the question whether these countries should be treated as democracies in the making, or as new authoritarian systems to be curbed.

FOCUS AND OBJECTIVES OF THIS STUDY

This study is not about theory, but it discusses a question that cannot be answered by simply looking at hard facts. The question is not whether the three countries are democratic, but whether the changes taking place at present in the political, economic, social, or any other realm are helping bring about conditions in which democracy may eventually develop. This is not a question that can be answered solely on the basis of factual information. The assumption underlying this discussion is that, in order to undergo a democratic transition, a country needs to accumulate capital first—not only the social capital discussed by Robert Putnam[8] but also the capital of power and authority that resides in the state, the economic and human capital that comes with development, and the institutional capital that may make democracy work in the long run. The most important question about Uganda, Ethiopia, and Eritrea is whether they are beginning to accumulate what can be called democratic capital.

The study provides an overview of Uganda, Eritrea, and Ethiopia, as well as a shorter discussion of Rwanda and the Democratic Republic of the Congo. The latter two countries are sometimes included in discussions of the new African leaders—correctly in the case of the former, incorrectly in that of the latter, and the contrast helps clarify what is different about the new leaders and their policies. Although the study focuses mostly on

---

8 Robert D. Putnam, *Making Democracy Work: Civic Traditions in Modern Italy* (Princeton, N.J.: Princeton University Press, 1992).

the domestic policies of these countries, it also considers their foreign policies, particularly their defiant attitude toward international and regional organizations and their determination, for better or for worse, to find African solutions to African problems.

In this discussion of the three countries, much attention is paid to their leaders—more so at times than to institutions, political parties, or social movements. This focus results not from the belief that history is always made by big men, but from the assessment that, in the particular situation of these countries, leadership is unusually important, more so than structural conditions, institutions, or organized forces. Structural conditions are the background against which all processes unfold, but they provide a better explanation of continuity than of change. Institutions and organized forces are very weak in all these countries. Leadership makes a difference—that is, ultimately, why the Democratic Republic of the Congo is not part of the model.

The present work is an attempt to apply scholarly analysis of modern Africa to important questions of current policy. Such questions typically do not lend themselves to clear-cut or definitive answers, and none such are offered in the pages that follow. The author hopes, however, that the combination of scholarly and policy analysis presented here will add a heretofore missing dimension to ongoing debates on how best to promote peace, stability, and prosperity in this troubled part of the world.

Chapter 2

THE BACKGROUND

A comparison of the policies of Uganda, Eritrea, and Ethiopia reveals the existence of a set of commonalities, rooted in the common challenge of reconstruction that the countries face. Some background is in order.

ETHIOPIA AND ERITREA

Ethiopia and Eritrea need to be discussed together initially, because until 1991 Eritrea was an Ethiopian province. Their history is unique in Africa. Never colonized except for a brief five years, Ethiopia before the revolution of 1974 was a feudal empire trying to evolve into a modern state in a process initiated and controlled from the top. The emperor sought to strengthen his power at the expense of the regional leaders while at the same time consolidating the borders of the old empire. The evolution was extremely uneven. The power of the central government increased, but it remained synonymous with that of the emperor—a master at creating alliances, co-opting potential opponents, and playing groups against each other to enhance his position. A rudimentary bureaucracy was set up, but it did not reach down to the local level. There were no mechanisms through which the population, or even segments of it, could hold the government accountable. The parliament was powerless, and political parties did not exist. There was, however, a large modern army, which enhanced the power of the emperor by freeing him from dependency on the feudal peasant armies raised in times of war by the landed class—a dependency that had persisted into the 1950s. Almost inevitably—in a country where no other institution was developed—the army emerged as the dominant force, overthrowing the emperor and seizing power in 1974. Thus, as a state, imperial Ethiopia was weak. Power depended on the emperor's capacity to create networks of

15

clients, not on the functioning of institutions. To the extent that Ethiopians had a national consciousness, it was the conscious-ness of subjects united under the emperor, not that of citizens with a voice in the government of the country.

Eritrea was an uneasy part of this system. An Italian colony after 1890, it was occupied by Britain in 1941 and administered by it (eventually under a U.N. mandate) until 1952, when the United Nations decided to federate it with Ethiopia, to which Eritrea had pre-colonial ties. The cohabitation between the feu-dal Ethiopian empire and the former colony could not work. The emperor was striving for absolute power, unshackled by the rights of regional rulers. Under foreign occupation, Eritrea had acquired a separate identity, although its population comprised the same mosaic of ethnic groups that inhabited northern Ethiopia. Furthermore, Eritrea had acquired the trappings of a modern state—including a functioning parliament and political parties. The emperor was not willing to cede to modern repre-sentative institutions any of the power he had been wresting away from the feudal class. In 1962, the federation was abol-ished; Eritrea lost its self-government and became a province of the empire. The result was the war for independence.

In 1974, the army seized power in Ethiopia. The radical officers, influenced by the ideas introduced in Ethiopia by the student movement, attempted to carry Ethiopia in one great leap across the chasm dividing an empire moving from feudal-ism to royal absolutism and the Marxist-Leninist state of which they dreamed. The model they had in mind was the Soviet one, both politically and economically. It required a strong, centrally controlled political party and a strong bureaucratic apparatus. Ethiopia had neither. It took the military ten years to establish a party. The bureaucratic machinery needed to impose centralized administration and economic control was never developed; and, despite attempts at collectivization, the economy remained dom-inated by subsistence agriculture. With the emperor's personal network of clients gone and the bureaucratic apparatus still weak, the military regime of Mengistu Haile Mariam could only control the country through repression. But repression was not an adequate tool to push through an ambitious project of social and economic transformation. The government had enough control to introduce some reforms, but not enough to consolidate them in the face of the inevitable resistance. Agricultural collectivization and peasant resettlement did not change the character of the rural economy, but they fueled discontent and increased support for opposition groups, eventually leading to civil war.

Opposition to the regime developed along two lines. The first, short-lived wave of opposition politics was rooted in groups based in the cities and led by urban intellectuals. Like the military, they wanted to transform the Ethiopian empire into a modern, centralized, bureaucratic, socialist state, but they could not accept that the military was implementing many of the reforms they had been advocating. These groups opposed the regime but not the state. They were eliminated within a few years. The second wave of opposition was dominated by ethnic liberation movements that threatened the state, not just the regime. These movements also shared the military's Marxist outlook. They did not ask for the right of individual citizens to elect their own government and to hold it accountable, but for the right of the ethnic groups that composed the Ethiopian population to control their own affairs. Rather than seek to reform the political system, the ethnic movements sought to reorganize the state drastically. To some, this meant breaking up the empire into independent nation-states; to others, it meant strong autonomy for each group. The already weak state was further weakened by this ethnic opposition, which called into question the legitimacy of Ethiopia in its imperial borders.

The resistance of the Eritrean nationalists intensified after 1974. Seeing the turmoil of the revolution as a major chance to attain their goal of independence, they escalated the fighting. By the mid-1980s, the guerrillas that the Ethiopian government used to dismiss as bandits had coalesced into an army capable of winning major victories on the battlefield. The infighting among rival nationalist movements, which had weakened their effectiveness, ceased as the Eritrean People's Liberation Front (EPLF) established its supremacy. The EPLF's goal was the independence of Eritrea, not the restructuring of the Ethiopian state—of which, it insisted, Eritrea had never been part until the United Nations arbitrarily decided otherwise. Yet the EPLF supported ethnic liberation movements in Ethiopia in order to weaken the state. The Tigrean People's Liberation Front (TPLF), fighting in

17

the small Tigray region immediately to the south of Eritrea, received the largest amount of assistance. Eritrean support, coupled with the determination and organizational ability of the TPLF's leadership, made it the most effective of the Ethiopian ethnic liberation movements.

The war waged by the EPLF and the TPLF, and to a much lesser extent the resistance of other organizations, finally defeated the military regime in May 1991. The TPLF entered Addis Ababa and set up a transitional government with the participation of other liberation movements as junior partners. The EPLF did not participate in this transitional government. Although EPLF officials agreed to a two-year waiting period before Eritrea became formally independent, they from the very beginning behaved as the leaders of a separate country—close to Ethiopia but having no right to participate, and no interest in participating, in its internal affairs.

Thus after May 1991 not only two new regimes but two new states came into existence in the area that had been the old Ethiopia. That Eritrea was a new state is obvious; that Ethiopia, too, was de facto a new state needs some explanation.[9] What made Ethiopia into a new state was not the loss of Eritrea—loss of territory by itself would not justify the statement—but the attempt by the TPLF to restructure the country completely, turning it from a centralized state into an ethnic federation. As an ethnic federation, Ethiopia was a new country that needed to develop new structures of government and new relations among its component parts. It thus faced the same problems as Eritrea. From the beginning, however, the two countries differed in one fundamental respect in their approach to building the state. Ethiopia decided to make ethnicity the basis for all political organizations and administrative structures. Eritrea, despite its nine ethnic groups in a population of about 3.5 million, decided that ethnicity had to be erased by strengthening a common national identity.

In their goal of making Ethiopia an ethnic federation, the TPLF leaders were strongly influenced by the Soviet model. Although by 1991 they had abandoned their commitment to

---

[9] See also Christopher Clapham, "Eritrean Independence and the Collapse of Ethiopian Centralism: Causes, Consequences and Implications," *Geopolitics and International Boundaries*, Vol. 1, 2, Autumn 1996, pp.115-29.

Marxism-Leninism, as had countless others around the world, their way of thinking had been shaped under the old ideology, and their belief in the right of nationalities to self-determination appeared unchanged. Pragmatic considerations also required a restructuring of the Ethiopian state. As an ethnic liberation movement representing a group that comprised at best 10 percent of the Ethiopian population, the TPLF could not hope to rule the country without facing the same ethnic revolts that had put an end to the previous regime. Having decided that Tigray should not secede, and having no intention to surrender power, the TPLF needed to reorganize the country in order to govern. The formation of an ethnic federation served such a purpose.

UGANDA

Uganda was very different. A British protectorate, it experienced an uneventful transition to independence in 1962. Relatively prosperous, it did not face a problem of economic viability. Its political viability, however, was another matter, because its population was both ethnically diverse and organized in political units with strong identities and claims. Britain had established its protectorate originally by negotiating an agreement with the Kingdom of Buganda, and it had subsequently recognized three more kingdoms and created a fourth. It had also subdivided the rest of the country, where traditional kingdoms did not exist and new ones were not plausible, into ethnically homogeneous districts ruled by so-called traditional chiefs. Despite these efforts to give all areas a degree of self-rule, Uganda remained subdivided into very unequal parts. The constitution of 1962 reflected the unequal ranking of local units, recognizing three different relations between central and local government. The Kingdom of Buganda had federal status, with a large sphere of autonomous power. The other kingdoms were given semi-federal status, with lesser autonomy, and inevitably aspired to full federal status. Finally, there were the simple districts, administrative units without a pre-colonial identity that nevertheless agitated for and obtained the right to choose a "constitutional head"—an ersatz traditional leader—so as to make their position more comparable to that of the kingdoms. It was a situation made for disaster, and disaster struck in the form of politics based on ethnic competition and ethnic conflict, first under civilian rule and later under a military government.

The first post-independence government had a parliamentary structure, with the king of Buganda recognized as its ceremonial president and Milton Obote, a member of the Langi ethnic group from the north, serving as prime minister. The alliance between Obote's Uganda People's Congress (UPC) and the Kabaka Yekka, the king's party, was a short-lived marriage of convenience contracted in order to defeat the Democratic Party (DP), which had unexpectedly won the pre-independence elections of 1961. The coalition did not last and neither did successive ones. In 1966, Obote tried to solve the problem by reorganizing the state in an attempt to curb ethnic politics.

A new constitution in 1966 curtailed the autonomy of the federal kingdoms and of the districts, and replaced the ceremonial president and prime minister with an executive president. A second constitution the following year went even further, dividing Buganda into four large districts and abrogating the official role of kings and constitutional heads of districts.

It was a pyrrhic victory for Obote. The new constitution formally downplayed ethnicity, but it also increased resentment, particularly among the Baganda. Moreover, as power was transferred to the center of the political system, the military became a more important political player. This both accentuated the north-south divide, as the military was dominated by northern groups, and increased the competition among the major northern ethnic groups—the Acholi, the Langi, and the Nubians. In 1971, Obote fell victim to a coup d'état spearheaded by General Idi Amin, a Nubian.

The narrow political base of Idi Amin and the incompetence of his rule led to the breakdown of the Ugandan state. Despite some initial popular measures, particularly the expulsion of the Asian community, his base of support progressively narrowed, first to the military and then to the Nubian soldiers within it. State terrorism became the tool that kept the government in power—fear and insecurity pervaded the country as thousands of people disappeared or fell victim to clumsily engineered accidents—but it eventually became insufficient. In 1979, with the intervention of the Tanzanian army, Idi Amin was forced from power, leaving behind a country devastated by economic mismanagement and divided by ethnic and regional conflict.

After a year of intense politicking, Milton Obote tried to stage a comeback but failed to consolidate his hold on the country. He was elected in the 1980 multi-party elections—the first the country had seen since independence—but the vote did not add to his legitimacy. On the contrary, it reaffirmed the continuation of ethnic divisions and their embeddedness in the political parties. The revived UPC emerged as the party of the northern groups; and the DP, as that of the south. Within months of the elections, Yoweri Museveni organized the National Resistance Army (NRA), drawing strong support in the south. After five years of warfare, the government army split along ethnic lines, with the Langi maintaining their support for Obote and the Acholi backing a coup d'état led by General Tito Okello. Obote was thus removed from power in July 1985. In January 1986, Museveni's NRA marched into Kampala.

The situation was dismal. The new leadership controlled the country militarily, but politically its hold was uneven. There was resentment among the groups that had dominated Obote's army, particularly the Acholi. There was little sense of an encompassing political community to which all Ugandan citizens belonged, and certainly no political institutions to govern that community, although there was a bloated and inefficient civil service that was more hindrance than help in reconstructing the country. The economy had been destroyed by the chaos of Amin's rule, by his expulsion of the Asian business community, and by five years of civil war. Thus Uganda, too, had to rebuild the state.

Indeed, the situation in 1986 was worse than it had been at independence. Thirty-five years of political crises had exacerbated ethnic cleavages. The divide between Protestants and Catholics, which had played a part around the time of independence, appeared less important, but Islam had become a potentially threatening political force. The kingdom of Buganda no longer existed, but the Baganda identity remained strong. The northern groups were deeply divided among themselves, each carrying different baggage—the Nubians their association with Idi Amin, the Langi theirs with Obote, and the Acholi theirs with

21

Okello, the general who had overthrown Obote in 1985 only to be defeated by Museveni a short time later. State institutions were also weaker; the British had left behind an administrative structure in better working order than the one of 1986. And after a period of a single-party system, Amin's dictatorship, a war, Obote's second period of rule, another coup, and a civil war, no political institutions to speak of remained.

THE CHALLENGE OF REBUILDING THE STATE

State collapse "refers to a situation where the structure, authority (legitimate power), law, and political order have fallen apart and must be reconstituted in some form, old or new."[10] Uganda in 1986 and Ethiopia in 1991 were collapsed states in which order had largely disintegrated. Eritrea was a new state. All three countries lacked both structure and legitimate authority—having only the power of the victorious military, the weak administrative structures of the previous regimes, and the non-state political organizations that the guerrilla movements had managed to develop during the war. The latter were strong in the areas longest under the movements' control but nonexistent in many others. In Eritrea, the EPLF political structure was relatively well-developed; the movement had strong leadership, it was disciplined, and it had the financial backing of Eritreans living abroad. Nevertheless, this was not adequate to govern a state. The challenge faced by the three countries was made more difficult by the economic situation. With economic activity at a standstill, the population impoverished, and tax collection mechanisms in disarray, state revenue was insufficient to finance even the most basic tasks. In all three countries, furthermore, there remained not only political opposition to the new regime but also pockets of armed resistance.

The legion of problems faced by the new governments in these countries emerging from civil war, state collapse, and economic disintegration can be divided schematically into three broad categories: the problem of power; the problem of authority, which (for reasons that will be explained below) includes eco-

---

[10] I. William Zartman, "Introduction: Posing the Problem of State Collapse," in I. William Zartman, ed., *Collapsed States: The Disintegration and Restoration of Legitimate Authority* (Boulder, Colo.: Lynne Rienner Publishers, 1995), p.1.

nomic rehabilitation; and the problem of participation. Solving the problems of power and authority meant rebuilding the state. Solving the problem of participation meant making it democratic. Only by tackling these problems with some measure of success could the new governments hope to survive and acquire legitimacy in the eyes of their citizens.

The Problem of Power

The problem of power comprises those tasks necessary to rebuilding the state in its most basic sense—that is, to establishing control over the entire territory and reasserting the government's monopoly over the means of coercion.

International recognition of the de jure sovereignty of the collapsed states of Uganda and Ethiopia presented no difficulty—in the late twentieth century, the international system paradoxically recognizes the territorial integrity and sovereignty even of states incapable of functioning as such. As for the Eritrean state, recognition of its sovereignty might have entailed a hard battle only a few years earlier, when African countries insisted on the inviolability of colonial borders and when the international community was extremely hesitant to accept modifications of post-World War II boundaries. By 1993, too many new countries had formed around the world, and in areas of much greater geopolitical importance, for the international community to object to the establishment of Eritrea. Furthermore, the ready acceptance of Eritrean independence by the new Ethiopian government made it impossible for other members of the Organization of African Unity not to go along.

The problem for the three countries was de facto sovereignty—that is, real control over the territory. This required establishing security by occupying the entire territory and by reducing the threat posed by armed groups. First and foremost, this meant demobilizing the remnants of the rival armies and militias, but it also involved reducing the size of the victorious armies. Developed to fight a war, these armies were far too large and too costly for peacetime purposes—and this also made them politically dangerous. Demobilizing the government's own army was a particularly delicate political task. Maintaining a very large one without a military mission was equally dangerous.

The Problem of Authority

Solving the problem of power was an essential first step, but a country is not governed through raw power alone, not comfortably at least, and probably not for long. Ethiopia, Eritrea, and Uganda confronted the problem of transforming the power that had ensured the victory of their new regimes into authority— into the administrative capacity to carry out the normal functions of government in a routine manner and without resorting to coercion, at least most of the time. They needed to develop not only the structures to maintain law and order without resorting to the army, but also those to keep schools open, repair roads, collect taxes, and perform in general the myriad services expected of a modern state.

This task of transforming power into authority required a functioning economy to provide citizens with sustenance and the government with revenue to carry out its functions without preying on the population and resorting to raw power. Reviving the economy in the three countries required both the rehabilitation of the existing statist apparatus, which was all they initially had, and the implementation of reforms aimed at liberalizing the economy—an absolute necessity if they wanted to obtain foreign assistance and debt rescheduling. Economic reform complicated political reform. At the beginning of the transition, private economic interest groups were weak in all three countries, while the bureaucracies controlling the economic apparatus were stronger. As economic reform progressed, new economic interest groups started developing in the private sector. Economic change thus also affected the nature of the political actors.

The Problem of Participation

The problem of participation is the most complex and multifaceted—and also the one bound to take the longest time to address. In brief, it requires moving from a situation where the country is controlled almost exclusively from the top—first through raw power, and then through the state's administrative structures—to one in which citizens also play a role. Participation can mean democracy in the Western sense of the word, but it also has other components and manifestations.

One aspect of participation is simply the development of a common identity among the citizens and thus their acceptance of the state as constituted. In the early post-colonial period, African leaders and outside observers alike put much emphasis on the concept of nation-building—that is, of developing a common national identity that would obliterate parochial attachments. Thirty years of ethnic politics have dispelled any illusion that ethnic identities can be easily overcome, making it even more imperative for all countries to negotiate a modus vivendi that allows all groups to remain part of a single state (Patrick Chabal calls this the building of an imagined political community).[11] Developing a political community is not, as the African founding fathers thought, a matter of teaching people to forget preexisting ethnic or religious identities, but one of negotiating an acceptable relationship between different groups and the state, as well as of defining the rights and duties of citizens vis-à-vis the government.

The challenge had different dimensions in each country. Ethiopia needed to give the politicized ethnic groups sufficient cultural space, autonomy in specific areas, and individual rights as citizens, to satisfy their identity; without these, they would not remain part of Ethiopia. Uganda needed to deal simultaneously with the existence of the old kingdoms as communities having their own identity and with the fears of the rest of the population. Eritrea had forged a strong political community of resistance against Ethiopia, but needed to find a new basis for community once it achieved independence and the former enemy turned into an ally.

The most difficult of the tasks to be accomplished, creating a political community, meant, first, solving the problem of individual and group participation in the political system. A second aspect of participation—in these countries as elsewhere—involved working out compromises among the political elites and giving these compromises an institutional form—broadening the regime with the creation of parliaments, regional administrations, or local governments, for example. Even when these institutions are not democratic, they broaden the basis of participation. A third necessary aspect was the further broadening of participation to include the entire population. International donors supporting political transformation in these countries

---

[11] See Patrick Chabal, *Power in Africa* (New York: St. Martin's Press, 1992), especially pp. 38-53.

believe that this requires competing political parties, autonomous organizations of civil society, and multi-party elections. The new leaders consider these to be vastly premature forms of participation, and they have sought to create different mechanisms, ranging from no-party elections in Uganda to national service for all young men and women in Eritrea. In some of these cases, participation entails a degree of choice for individuals, and thus elements of democracy—as in the case of no-party elections. In others, it entails becoming part of a collective effort, without any element of choice—in other words, mobilization orchestrated from the top. The tension between mobilization and genuine participation remains strong in all three countries.

While in theory the lines separating power, authority, and participation are fairly clear, in practice there is a lot of overlap among them. Government authority is always ultimately backed up by power—and the line is particularly difficult to draw in the case of governments that have come to power through force in the first place. The problem of authority cannot always be separated from that of participation: establishing a viable administrative structure is not purely a technical exercise to be conducted on the basis of efficiency and rationality, but also a political exercise that defines identity and forms of participation. Ethiopia, for example, has designed its administrative districts to be ethnically homogeneous, and Eritrea, to be heterogeneous—with clear implications for participation.

The distinction between power, authority, and participation is important nonetheless, in view of the tendency of international donors to assume that participation is the cure-all for a country's political problems. It is also helpful in analyzing how the new leaders have handled the task of reconstituting the state and the political regime.

WHAT KIND OF TRANSITION?

Uganda, Ethiopia, and Eritrea have been quite successful—relative to the conditions from which they started—in reconstructing mechanisms of authority. The countries are being governed again; normal life is possible over much of the territory; laws are made and implemented; and the economy has revived beyond all expectations. This does not mean that the three countries do not still face enormous problems, or do not have a long way to go before they can be considered stable modern states. But it is undeniable that change has been for the better.

Progress in solving the problem of participation has been much slower. The three governments have attempted to redefine their relationship with the various groups, but mostly have done so unilaterally rather than in consultation with those groups. Mechanisms for participation and inclusion remain rudimentary. In Ethiopia and Uganda in particular, some groups still reject the political community as defined from the center, and even wage armed resistance.

Finally, none of the mechanisms on which the governments have relied to run the country can yet be considered institutionalized. They are still new, in flux, subject to unilateral change. To some extent, this is simply a function of time. In part, it also depends on the magnitude of the task. The problem remains, and the disappearance of the leaders at this point could still result in the undoing of much of what has been accomplished so far. The three countries are indeed caught in a vicious circle in this respect: the absence of institutions enhances the role of the leaders—in fact makes strong leadership a necessity. But strong leadership, in turn, could become a hindrance to the development of institutions, and it could be corrupted into personal rule.

Chapter 3

UGANDA AND THE POLITICS OF PROCESS

When Museveni fought his way into Kampala in 1986, he inherited a country marked by the old ethnic and regional divisions that had caused conflict since independence as well as further embittered by the massacres of the Amin period and of the brutal war between the National Resistance Army and Obote's Ugandan National Liberation Army (UNLA). An estimated 400,000 people (of a population of about 12 million in 1980) had died in each of these two periods. Unless a way could be found to reconcile the segments of the population that had been fighting each other in the past, there was no hope for peace. Museveni's policies therefore focused on restoring the unity of the country and the structures of the state. Democracy, he claimed, would come later.

Since 1986, the Ugandan state has been largely restored, although security remains a problem in parts of the north and west. Deep divisions remain, however, as the country prepares to decide in a referendum in 2000 whether it should take the final step toward becoming a multi-party electoral democracy. Crisscrossing the old ethnic and economic cleavages are new divisions between those looking at politics as a matter of absolute principles and those looking at it as a matter of process. The best hope for the country is that the politics of process will prevail over the politics of high principles.

In 1986, the new government created by the National Resistance Army and its political wing, the National Resistance Movement (NRM), confronted urgent problems of power and authority. It had to restore security, that is, to establish the monopoly over use of force that is one of the characteristics of the modern state; and it had to make the transition from mili-

29

tary to political control, strengthening the top-down institutions for administering the country and implementing decisions taken by the government. Such institutions in turn could not be developed unless the economy revived, providing the revenue to finance the activities of the government. These were the minimal tasks needed to restore a stable system resting on control from the top.

Solving the problem of participation was less urgent, from the point of view of the government. A democratic transformation of the resurrected state required: electoral institutions that allowed citizens to choose and dismiss government officials, making them accountable; complex government institutions that allowed agencies to restrain each other; political parties that made the act of voting meaningful by presenting the citizens with choices among candidates and policies; and civil society organizations contributing to the pluralism of the system by advocating the policy reform that would most benefit their constituents. These were not tasks the government could accomplish alone. The future of Uganda—the difference between a democratic transition and a return to conflict and state collapse—depended not only on the reforms instituted by the Museveni government, but also on the evolution of the society and its political and social organizations.

Reconstruction was made more difficult by the fundamental flaws of the Ugandan state: a combination of politicized ethnicity, reflected in the sectarian nature of the political parties and the continuing resistance to the government among the Acholis; tension between the more developed south and the less developed north, which unfortunately coincided with the division between the groups that had given most support to the NRA and those from which the UNLA had been recruited; and the twilight existence of the Kingdom of Buganda, which could be neither ignored as if it had never existed nor recognized formally as a federal state without stirring up a host of problems.

Museveni was starting from a position of weakness. Many saw the NRM as a southern rather than a national organization. It had originated in the southwestern part of the country, and a disproportionate number of its cadres came from there. The region had taken the brunt of the fighting, but it nevertheless continued to support the NRM. The rudimentary government institutions that the movement had been able to set up before 1986 were also stronger there. The Uganda National Liberation Army against which Museveni fought had recruited mostly in the north. The new government thus needed to live down the perception that its victory would lead to southern domination and the marginalization of the north. It never did so completely.

The NRM did not have a blueprint on how to approach these problems when it came to power. Like most political organizations in Africa at the time, it was in a transitional period ideologically and politically. The socialist or even Marxist-Leninist ideals upheld by many African leaders and intellectuals of the first post-independence generation were being questioned, but the suspicion of the alternatives proposed by the West remained great. Museveni embodied the ideological dilemma. Educated at the University of Dar-es-Salaam at a time when few African intellectuals would consider calling themselves anything other than socialist, he came to power after the failure of the African economies and the drying up of Soviet aid had left governments little choice but to accept the reforms imposed by the international financial institutions. In 1986, however, the Cold War was not yet over, and international donors did not insist on democracy, much less had they codified the concept of a democratic transition into a series of simple steps for every country to follow. Museveni was free to chart a new course.

The Ten Point Programme, the NRM's pre-1986 charter, offered little guidance. It called for: the restoration of democracy and of security; the consolidation of national unity and the elimination of all forms of sectarianism; the defense and consolidation of national independence; the building of an independent, integrated, and self-sustaining national economy; the restoration and improvement of social services and the rehabilitation of war-ravaged areas; the elimination of corruption and the misuse of power; redress of errors that resulted in the dislocation of some sections of the population; cooperation with other African countries; and the development of a mixed economy. More than a program, it was a list of problems that needed attention.[12]

The policies of the new government were in the end guid-

[12] *What Is Africa's Problem: Speeches and Writing on Africa by Yoweri Kaguta Museveni* (Kampala: NRM Publications, 1992), p. 279 ff.

31

ed by political pragmatism and fear of renewed conflict. Fear of party politics in particular went very deep for Museveni. It was more than a self-serving attitude—though of course not having to compete in open elections against other political organizations did not hurt the NRM's chances of staying in power. The old Ugandan political parties had been divisive, sectarian organizations in the first Obote government, and had turned immediately into divisive, sectarian organizations in the 1980s, with the UPC coming back to power in fraudulent elections. After the NRM victory in 1986, the more moderate elements of all parties joined the Museveni government, leaving the organizations in the hands of leaders less likely to seek reconciliation and compromise. Museveni's fear of political parties was understandable, and much of the population, particularly in rural areas badly affected by conflict in the past, shared the view that competition might degenerate into conflict.

REBUILDING THE STATE

The first tasks the government confronted in 1986 were the restoration of security and the establishment of normal government and administration. It was able to restore security in most of the country fairly quickly and to set up new and much stronger administrative structures within a few years. But considerable areas of conflict remained in part of the north and west, the result of a combination of domestic discontent and external intervention from the Sudan and the eastern Congo. By 1998, security was again worsening, raising the possibility that the progress made in the rebuilding of the administration and the economy would also be undermined.

Strengthening Power

The National Resistance Army was the key to the restoration of the Ugandan state. It was the tool that had allowed Museveni to defeat Obote and Okello, but it needed to be brought firmly under civilian control and to be depoliticized if the new regime was going to be different from previous ones. In addition to the NRA, which was a fairly disciplined body, the government had to contend with the defeated Ugandan National Liberation Army (UNLA), an undisciplined, faction-ridden organization described by a Ugandan scholar as "no more than the arithmetic summation of various competing semi-private armies."[13] The UNLA, as mentioned earlier, had split in 1985 when the Acholis in its ranks supported Tito Okello and the Langis took Obote's side.[14]

Museveni dealt with these armies as he did with the political parties: he opened the ranks of the NRA to their men as he opened his cabinet to leaders of other parties, as long as they joined as individuals and not as representatives of organizations or as part of a military unit (an early attempt to accept entire units caused much friction and was abandoned). By absorbing the soldiers of rival armies in the NRA, the government reduced the immediate danger posed by the large number of armed men who had no source of livelihood in the devastated country other than their weapons, but it also burdened itself with a very large military establishment. In 1986, it was estimated that the NRA had 14,000 men under its command. By 1990, an army of 80,000 was draining 31 percent of the budget. Beginning in late 1992, with the help of the World Bank, a demobilization program reduced the army to 50,000 and military expenditure to 16 percent of the budget.[15] Thus, in a ten-year process, Uganda succeeded first in absorbing rival combatants into the NRA and then in reducing the overall size of the military through a donor-supported program that helped the demobilized soldiers reintegrate into civilian life—a significant accomplishment. On the negative side, however, the military became quite corrupt at the top, with the involvement of members of Museveni's family.

Putting an end to armed resistance in the north, in particular among the Acholis, also proved difficult. The problem of northern resistance was not created by Museveni. Like many intractable African problems, it was a product of discriminatory colonial policies that favored the south over the north and of thirty years of post-independence mismanagement of ethnic relations. But Museveni did not succeed in solving it.

---

[13] Mahmood Mamdani, "Uganda in Transition: Two Years of the NRA/NRM," *Third World Quarterly*, Vol. 10, 3, July 1988, p.1159.
[14] See E.A. Brett, "Neutralising the Use of Force in Uganda: The Role of the Military in Politics," *Journal of Modern African Studies*, Vol. 33, 1, 1995, pp. 129-52.
[15] Nat Colletta and Nicole Ball, "War to Peace Transition in Uganda," *Finance and Development*, Vol. 30, 3, June 1993, p. 36 ff. ; and "Demobilization and Reintegration of Military Personnel in Africa: The Evidence from Seven Country Case Studies," Discussion Paper, Africa Regional Series, The World Bank, October 1993.

In 1987, popular discontent erupted in the form of the Holy Spirit Movement, a millenarian movement called into existence by a young woman named Alice Lakwena. A mixture of northern, particularly Acholi, nationalism and moral crusade, bolstered by a combination of religious faith and belief in magic, the Holy Spirit Movement embarked on what Lakwena claimed was a God-ordained mission to oust the government. Poorly armed and organized, the Holy Spirit Movement nevertheless survived for a year through the fervor of its followers, fought many bloody battles with the army, and managed to march through a considerable section of the country before being defeated. The cost was high, not only for the Movement's followers but generally for the civilian population of the northern areas.[16]

The defeat of the Holy Spirit Movement was followed by the rise of another organization, the Lord Resistance Army of Joseph Kony. Despite its name, the LRA was less a continuation of Lakwena's crusade than a political organization entangled in the enmity between the Sudan and Uganda and the latter's fear of the Khartoum government's support for Islamist organizations in other countries. The tension between the two countries led Kampala to support the Sudanese People's Liberation Army (SPLA) against Khartoum, and Khartoum to support the LRA against Kampala. With outside support and safe bases in the Sudan, the LRA could not be easily defeated like the Holy Spirit Movement, but an attempt in 1994 to negotiate an agreement failed, leaving the two sides to seek a military solution. All reports indicated that the LRA resorted to extremely brutal tactics, particularly the kidnapping of children and their use as porters, sex objects, and cannon fodder.[17] The violence against the local population and the gross human rights abuses committed by the LRA reduced its support among the northern population, but without increasing support for the government, which remained unable to provide security in the affected areas.[18] The

---

[16] Amii Omara-Otunnu, "The Struggle for Democracy in Uganda," *Journal of Modern African Studies*, Vol. 30, 3, 1992, pp. 443-63.

[17] U.S. Department of State Bureau of Democracy, Human Rights and Labor, "Uganda Country Report on Human Rights Practices for 1997," January 1998. Reports for earlier years show a very similar pattern.

[18] A USAID-funded study documents well the alienation of the population from both the LRA and the Museveni government. See Robert Gersony, "The Anguish of Northern Uganda: Results of a Field-Based Assessment of the Civil Conflict in Northern Uganda" (Kampala, Uganda: USAID Mission to Uganda, 1997).

western border area also remained troubled, with domestic tensions exacerbated by the conflict in Rwanda and the close relationship between Museveni and Paul Kagame.

The failure by the Museveni government to solve the problem of security remains one of the most troubling, dangerous problems Uganda faces. The military has been ineffectual against the insurgents, but it has created resentment among the population of the affected areas, which remains mired in a vicious circle of conflict and poverty, unable to partake of the progress being made elsewhere. To make matters worse, the situation in the west will probably deteriorate further as a result of Uganda's deepening involvement in the domestic conflict in the Democratic Republic of the Congo and of the increasing chaos in the eastern region of that country, bordering on Uganda (this will be discussed further in Chapter 7). In turn, a growing security problem risks undermining the progress made in rebuilding a system of government and administration.

Creating Institutions of Authority

When the NRM marched into Kampala, it took over a capital city and a set of government buildings, but not a viable system of government. The state had collapsed, leaving in its wake organizations used to operating with a high degree of autonomy and outside a framework of legality and accountability. There was no police system on which the government could rely, for example, but there were police and military units, or intelligence services, that were not under control.[19] The NRM had the power that came from its military superiority, but that was not enough to govern. The new leadership had the good will of the urban intelligentsia but a narrow base of support. In rural areas, it could count only on a very sketchy system of local Resistance Councils (RCs) set in place during the war in the limited area it controlled; to implement policy, it depended on the remains of the civil service—historically one of the best in Africa but now bloated, underpaid, disorganized, and demoralized.

To consolidate a system of government, Museveni tried to broaden the regime by reaching out to other parties, extended

---

[19] For more, see Anthony J. Regan, "Constitutional Reform and the Politics of the Constitution in Uganda: A New Path to Constitutionalism?" in P. Langseth, J. Katorobo, E. Brett, and J. Munene, eds., *Uganda: Landmarks in Rebuilding a Nation* (Kampala: Fountain Publishers, 1995) pp. 160-61.

the local RCs to all parts of the country, and sought to reform the civil service. Underpinning the effort was the attempt to rehabilitate the economy, not only to improve the livelihood of the population but also to generate the financial means to support an effective system of government.

In Museveni's original promise, the transitional period of NRM control from the top was to last only four years, after which there were to be elections. The transitional period was extended on the ground that the problems in the north had slowed down the needed reforms. As a result, the first presidential elections did not take place until 1996, ten years after the NRM victory and after a new constitution finally had been enacted. Elections for local councils first took place in 1987, however, and those for the National Resistance Council—the interim legislative assembly—in 1989.

The Museveni government had sympathizers in much of the country, but its organized political base was weak. To broaden it, Museveni co-opted personalities from other political organizations, particularly the Democratic Party. He did not form a government of national reconciliation in the strict sense of the term, because such a government is based on an agreement among political parties, and Museveni refused to recognize a legitimate role for the political parties in the interim period. Rather, he attempted to broaden the NRM into the all-encompassing movement he wanted it to be. The parties, which became known collectively as the "multiparties," were not forcibly disbanded, and they continued to maintain offices in Kampala, to publish newspapers, and even to present candidates for election, although not officially. They were not, however, allowed to hold meetings, to recruit members, or to campaign openly.

The strengthening of the Resistance Council (RC) system also received immediate attention. Local RCs were first elected during the war on an ad hoc basis in the areas under NRM control, particularly in the Luwero triangle, where the fighting first started. Their authority originally was simply determined by what they could achieve in the power vacuum of the collapsed state. In general, the councils appear to have been well received, since they gave the population some control over local government. After 1986, RCs were set up in all regions, and their position was formally defined. Local government statutes enacted in 1987-88 created a five-tier system of Resistance Councils, starting at the village level and culminating with the district level, and defined the authority and functions of each.[20]

Elections for the RCs were first held not by secret ballot but by the totally public queuing system, with voters lining up in front of the chosen candidate's picture. Elections to the successive levels were indirect, with each level of councils sending delegates up to the next level. It was a cheap and easy form of voting, suited to the conditions prevailing initially. It also lent itself well to what the government wanted—no-party elections, in which voters would presumably focus on the merits of the individual candidates and not on their party affiliations. The voters' direct control, however, was limited to the village level. In 1998, direct elections by secret ballot were held for the first time for all levels of local government, up to the district level.[21] The 1998 local elections are notable because almost three-quarters of the incumbents were voted out of office, mostly because of corruption and incompetence. This shows both the difficulty of creating honest and effective local government and the fact that decentralization really helps enhance accountability.

The RCs have thus been transformed over a twelve-year period from wartime, makeshift organizations into a decentralized system of government. New statutes have given the councils, particularly at the district level, additional control over budgetary matters and over personnel previously controlled by the ministries. While the capacity of local councils remains weak and their financial resources limited, local government reform is an important component of the restructuring of the state in Uganda. Museveni's critics in the so-called multiparties, however, see decentralization as a poor substitute for the federal system that Uganda had under its first constitution.

---

[20] Per Tidemand, "New Local State Forms and 'Popular Participation' in Buganda, Uganda," in Peter Gibbon, ed., *The New Local Level Politics in East Africa* (Uppsala: Scandinavian Institute of African Studies, 1994), pp. 22-49; Anthony J. Regan, "A Comparative Framework for Analysis of Uganda's Decentralization Policy," in P. Langseth et al., op. cit., pp. 271-303; Expedit Ddungu, "Popular Forms and the Question of Democracy: The Case of Resistance Councils in Uganda," in Mahmood Mamdani and Joe Oloka-Onyango, eds., *Uganda: Studies in Living Conditions, Popular Movements, and Constitutionalism* (Vienna: Jeep Books, 1993), pp. 365-403.

[21] The exceptions were the elections of candidates to the one-third of seats reserved for women in all councils. These seats were filled by the queuing system, resulting in low voter turnout and much criticism by the election-monitoring NGOs.

The restructuring of the civil service has been more halting than the reform of local government. As part of the economic structural adjustment program, the government has taken steps to reduce the number of civil servants, trying to eliminate ghost workers from the payroll and retrenching others. Progress, however, has been slow. Furthermore, corruption has re-emerged as a serious problem under the Museveni government.

Strengthening the Economy

The rehabilitation of the economy has been a major success, on the other hand, winning Uganda high praise from the IMF and the World Bank and probably decreasing international pressure on Museveni to carry out more rapid political reform.

Initial economic policy was uncertain at best. In 1986, the NRM displayed traces of the broadly socialist orientation still common among African political movements at the time. The Ten Point Programme advocated the development of a mixed economy, implying an important role for the state sector. Indeed, in the early months, the Museveni government was pulled in two conflicting directions: the revival of the old statist system, or transformation into a market economy.[22] The latter trend eventually won out, and the government made a strong commitment to economic reform.

Beginning in 1987, the government launched an economic recovery program supported by the IMF, the World Bank, and bilateral donors. Immediate goals were to bring inflation and budget deficits under control as well as to rehabilitate the infrastructure. Longer-term goals included the promotion of exports, increasing agricultural productivity through the liberalization of agricultural markets, and efforts to attract more foreign investment. It was, in other words, a classical stabilization and structural adjustment approach. What made Uganda unusual was the government's firm commitment to the reform process and the degree of success it achieved. By 1994, Uganda had achieved an average growth rate of 6 percent a year for six years.[23] Growth rates have been even higher in the following years, although they started tapering off by 1998.

[22] E. A. Brett, "Rebuilding Organizational Capacity in Uganda Under the National Resistance Movement," *Journal of Modern African Studies*, Vol. 32, 1, 1994, pp. 53-80.
[23] International Monetary Fund, *Uganda: Adjustment with Growth, 1987-94*, Occasional Paper 121 (Washington, D.C.: IMF, March 1995).

The early uncertainty about economic policy and the role of the state was soon replaced by enthusiastic commitment to economic liberalization. A sign of such commitment was the decision to invite back the members of the Asian community expelled by Idi Amin in 1972. The departure of the Asians had been a blow for Uganda, contributing to the economic collapse of the Amin period. Many Asians responded to Museveni's invitation and returned, bringing to Uganda badly needed capital and managerial expertise.

Despite these positive trends, economic problems remain very serious. Dependence on agriculture is great, and government revenue remains low, in part due to the difficulty of collecting taxes. Privatization engendered growth but also fueled corruption. The gap between the more developed south and the north is wide and likely to grow even wider because of the continuing conflict and because private-sector investors are more concerned with profits than with promoting regional balance. In addition, the IMF and World Bank loans that have helped Uganda reform its economy also have turned it into one of the most highly indebted countries in Africa. Despite the remarkable growth rates achieved in recent years, Uganda's economy is still fragile and will remain so for a long time even under a best-case scenario. Recovery from economic devastation is a slow process.

INCREASING PARTICIPATION

One issue that sharply divides Ugandans among themselves, and Uganda from the donor community, is democratization. Museveni believes that his government has already taken many steps toward building a political system that allows participation by all citizens, and that it is laying the groundwork that will allow it to develop a formal, competitive, multi-party system. The "multiparties" argue that the banning of political parties is an inexcusable violation of the fundamental freedom of association, and that it is absurd to talk of democracy as long as this situation continues. Donors increasingly believe that Uganda is running out of excuses to postpone the holding of multi-party elections—and thereby its transition to democracy. In 1986, the argument that Uganda needed time to stabilize the situation and to reconstruct state institutions was credible; in 1998, it looks suspiciously like the beginning of the slippery road toward authoritarianism. The intermediate ground is occupied by many Ugandan NGOs that believe they can achieve, in the words of one of their officials, "democratization by stealth"—not by insisting on the immediate acceptance of multi-party democracy, but by pushing the government into enacting fundamental reforms. They see such a process of incremental reform as more productive than a confrontation on absolute principles.

Museveni defends his views with a simple and to some extent plausible argument. Uganda is still so divided by the events of its first thirty years that it cannot move immediately toward competitive, multi-party democracy. The political parties are tainted with the legacy of the past. They are not divided by ideological and programmatic differences, which would lead people to vote along class lines, on the basis of interests that are relatively fluid and subject to change; instead, they are pitted against each other by ethnic and religious differences, which are rigid and consequently dangerous. Uganda thus cannot yet embrace multi-partyism. Instead, it needs a "movement system," with an all-embracing organization that promotes reconciliation rather than divisions. Under the movement system, which critics call a single-party system, citizens can vote in competitive elections. However, they choose not among parties but among individuals. Since anyone can run for office, this is not a single-party system.

Museveni's claim that a movement system can be democratic is supported to some extent by the relative openness of Uganda. The parties are suspended but not banned, and their members become candidates in the elections, although they can only campaign as individuals rather than as representatives of a party. Important political offices, including the mayoralty of Kampala, are won by "multi-partyists" rather than by "movementists." Furthermore, the media are quite free—not only the printed media but radio as well, with FM radio stations broadcasting political call-in talk shows and debates in which political parties are freely mentioned and their positions discussed. Publishing in general is also quite free—indeed, many of the publications expressing critical views of the Museveni regime consulted in carrying out this study were published in Kampala.

Uganda's human rights record remains a matter of much dissension. To some, the banning of political parties is a serious violation in itself, and the government deserves international censure. Others look at the whole situation and find the record fair. Many problems are caused by insufficient state capacity and levels of training (for example, by local police overstepping the boundaries of their mandate and carrying out tasks that should be left to the national police); few represent the deliberate perpetration of human rights violations by officials who know full well what they are doing (for example, people do not disappear).[24]

The twelve years of Museveni's rule have also seen the development of some institutions necessary for democracy, although others are lagging far behind. The drafting and approval of a new constitution were crucial to the development of such institutions—less because of what the constitution says than because of the way in which it was drafted. The NRM operated initially under an amended version of the 1967 constitution. In 1989, the government appointed a constitutional commission, known as the Odoki Commission, to prepare a new charter. After many delays, the commission submitted a draft in 1993. A constituent assembly was elected in 1994 in competitive but no-party elections, and it approved the constitution the following year. Presidential and parliamentary elections followed in 1996. It was a leisurely process: Museveni competed in an election for the first time ten years after the NRM had come to power.

The slowness was explained in part by the broad process of consultation carried out by the Odoki Commission. This consultation may have been more important for the future of democracy in Uganda than the content of the constitution. There are many ways to prepare a constitution. One is to put the task in the hands of experts—as was done in much of Africa at the time of independence, for example. Another is to negotiate a political compromise among the major political forces in the country and to draft a constitution that reflects that agreement—essentially the process followed in South Africa between 1990 and 1994. Uganda chose yet another approach: the constitutional commis-

---

[24] See, for example, U.S. Department of State, "Uganda Country Report on Human Rights Practices for 1997," op. cit.

sion consulted the population at large, in a series of meetings held throughout the country, and drafted a constitution purportedly representing the views expressed in the consultation. This method—which was also followed in Eritrea and to a lesser extent in Ethiopia—could have turned into a simple exercise in mobilizing the population behind the government through a mock process of consultation. The fact that the political parties could not participate as parties could easily have turned the consultation into a meaningless exercise. The fact that it did not do so was the result of the determination of many organizations of civil society, particularly human rights and women's NGOs, to take advantage of all opportunities to make sure the constitution helped advance their goals.

The Odoki Commission organized dozens of meetings just to identify the issues to be discussed by the public, then prepared and very widely distributed educational material concerning those issues, and finally convened hundreds of meetings—at least one in most of the over 900 sub-counties—in which individuals and organizations were invited to comment orally and to submit written comments. Almost 25 percent of villages submitted written comments, showing both the scope of the exercise and the vitality of the local Resistance Councils.[25] Many NGOs also played a crucial role.

The most controversial issues in the discussion were inevitably the political ones. Two in particular received much attention: the choice between a multi-party and a "movement" system; and the decision as to whether to give recognition to traditional rulers—that is, whether the kingdoms should be restored and Uganda should revert to something similar to the curious federation of 1962, which incorporated kingdoms in a republican state.

A compromise was reached in both cases. The constitution recognizes the legitimacy of both the movement system and the multi-party system. As long as the movement system prevails, parties have the right to exist but not to participate officially in the elections. The 1996 elections were held under the movement system; in the year 2000, the population is expected to decide in a referendum whether the 2001 elections will also be held under

---

[25] Anthony J. Regan, "Constitutional Reform . . . ," op. cit.

42

the movement system, or whether they will mark the transition to multi-party democracy.

Traditional authorities receive official recognition in the constitution, but only as cultural figures with no political powers and no right to run for office. This means that Uganda remains a unitary state, instead of reverting to a federal or even semi-federal constitution, but that the kings retain a role. In 1993, the king of Buganda was crowned with great ceremony, and the others soon followed the example. Like all compromises, the solution has not satisfied anyone entirely. Many Baganda would have preferred to restore the kingdom as a federal state. Other groups worried that even the limited recognition of kings as cultural symbols would be enough to rekindle the old conflicts. That the government has no intention of recognizing the kingdoms or allowing the open ethnicization of politics has been made clear by the ban on ethnic and other sectarian parties. But it is also a sign of the times that a government that has banned ethnic parties has felt compelled to give some recognition to the country's cultural and ethnic diversity.

Several other important issues have caused less controversy but have had considerable impact nevertheless. One concerns the position of women in Uganda. The constitution recognizes equal rights for women, including the right to own and inherit land—hardly unusual in a late twentieth-century constitution. But this is just the beginning of the process. The constitution also sets aside seats for women in all elected bodies, in an attempt to break the cultural resistance to women's participation in public affairs. A network of NGOs continues to work to ensure that the broad constitutional provisions will be given substance by the enactment of the necessary laws. The NGOs are ready to admit that a lot more needs to be done. They feel, however, that they can accomplish much in this and many other areas even before the multi-party system is introduced. One of the results of the consultation that surrounded the preparation of the constitution has been the growth of a culture of incremental reform rather than one of absolute principles.

Although it has legalized the non-democratic "movement" system, the Ugandan constitution contains many strong democratic features, including extensive checks and balances in the government, some pluralism of representation, and accountabil-

43

ity even in the absence of multi-partyism. Power is dispersed both horizontally (among executive agencies) and vertically (between the central government and local ones). The constitution provides for many independent agencies with oversight power over the executive: the Human Rights Commission, the Office of the Inspector General (ombudsman), the Audit Commission, the Director of Public Prosecutions, the Inspector General of Police, the Electoral Commission, the Board of the Central Bank, the Public Service Commission. Within a few years, some of these agencies, particularly the Inspector General's office, have become well established and are seen as both independent and effective. The constitution has also dispersed power vertically by confirming and strengthening the role of local government. All told, the constitution has not created a monolithic system despite the absence of party competition.[26]

The weaknesses of the emerging system are also evident. Democratic space still depends excessively on the good will of the NRM and of President Museveni, because there are no political forces strong enough to force the government to move, should it decide it does not want to make further concessions. The opposition parties remain extremely weak and, above all, seemingly mired in the past. The responsibility for the weakness of the political parties is not entirely their own, since they are prevented from organizing freely. On the other hand, they are not completely deprived of political space—the press freely reports on the statements of their leaders and their activities. Rather, they appear to have decided not to avail themselves of the limited space that is available in order to fight for more. Instead, they demand that the government open up all the space immediately. They have no choice but to boycott the referendum on the transition to a multi-party system, they argue, because freedom of association is an absolute right and thus cannot be put to a vote. While NGOs are busy pressing the government to carry out more reforms, the parties demand that Museveni give in unconditionally, or that the donors force him to do so by withholding aid; the alternative, they warn, would be renewed violence. Like many other opposition parties in Africa, the "multi-parties" appear to be playing the politics of absolute principles

---

[26] See Anthony J. Regan, ibid.

without achieving very much, while NGOs, focusing on process, are bringing about some change.

Had the NRM been a monolithic movement, and had Museveni shown a more authoritarian bent, neither the clauses of the constitution nor the pressure from the NGOs—typical small, urban-based, elite African NGOs—would have sufficed to prevent the movement system from crystallizing into an old-fashioned single-party system. But the NRM is indeed a broad movement, and Museveni is willing to tolerate diverse opinions, particularly when they do not threaten him directly. Furthermore, a growing number of movement supporters have become convinced of the necessity of completing the transition to a multi-party system even without waiting for the referendum in the year 2000. The diversity of ideas within the movement strengthens the democratic features of the regime by making the NRM–controlled parliament a lively organization not prepared to rubber-stamp government decisions. A controversial land bill proposed by the government in 1998—providing, among other things, for the transfer of some land from absentee landowners to long-term tenants—has been at the center of a heated debate, widely publicized by the press and on radio, before being voted into law.

But there are signs of danger as well. The 1996 parliamentary elections have provided evidence that the NRM is not immune from the temptations of uncontested power. As an all-encompassing movement, the NRM is supposed to be neutral toward the candidates competing in the elections and committed only to ensuring that the voters receive the information they need to cast their vote in a rational way. Too often, however, it has acted as a political party seeking the election of its own candidates and the exclusion of others; it has even represented the outcome as an elections victory—an oxymoron for a movement that supposedly represents everybody.[27]

CONCLUSIONS

Since 1986, Uganda has undergone remarkable and mostly positive change. The Ugandan state has been restored to a large extent, with sufficient order and administrative structures

---

27 See Mikael Karlström, "Imagining Democracy: Political Culture and Democratization in Buganda," *Africa*, Vol. 66, 4, 1996, esp. pp. 498-500.

to allow daily life and economic activity to unfold in a normal way in most of the country. The healthy rate of economic growth testifies to this restoration of normality as well as to the restructuring of the economy. With a streamlined military, a viable framework for local government, and a constitution arrived at through a consultative process, Uganda has also started to strengthen the institutional framework of the state.

The human rights record of the government has improved considerably. Reports suggest that the main problems result from the weakness of the institutions.[28] But freedoms of association and speech are still curtailed by the ban on party activities. Armed opposition still exists and is probably increasing in the north and along the western border—to some extent as a spillover of conflicts in neighboring countries, but also because of a reservoir of discontent that the government appears incapable or unwilling to address.

Not only is Uganda not democratic, but its progress remains reversible—with its political stability threatened by continuing armed opposition in parts of the country and by the possibility of renewed crisis in the entire region, and with its economic recovery still at risk (as in all recovering African countries) because of the magnitude of the problems. Leadership remains more important than institutions. Although this is perhaps inevitable after only ten years, it creates a very dangerous situation. In all areas, however, a process of change is still under way.

---

[28] U.S. Department of State, "Uganda Country Report on Human Rights Practices for 1997," op. cit.

Chapter 4

ERITREA: COMMAND STATE AND MARKET ECONOMY

The last new state in Africa, Eritrea officially attained independence in 1993, although all Ethiopian control effectively ceased in May 1991. Officials of the Eritrean People's Liberation Front (EPLF) portrayed the victory as the last chapter in the decolonization of Africa—the attainment of independence by a colony that had wrongfully been denied the right to self-determination in the past. But others saw the independence of Eritrea as the first manifestation of the post–Cold War African order, in which colonial boundaries were no longer sacred. The foreign policy of Eritrea, discussed later, lends credibility to this interpretation.

Eritrea was not only a new state in the juridical sense, it was also a surprisingly new country from the administrative, and to some extent the economic, points of view. The Ethiopian political, administrative, and military apparatus collapsed entirely in May 1991. However, while Ethiopia had to contend with the remnants of the old regime—the soldiers of the defeated army, the officials of the former administration and political party— Eritrea did not. The frightened Ethiopians vanished over the border or were forcibly repatriated by the EPLF—some 200,000 were trucked to the border and left there. Countries like Mozambique and Angola, which had seen a similar sudden collapse of the old institutions and the sudden departure of the old personnel, suffered grievously because of it, never quite recovering. Eritrea had a much easier time, because it already had at least a rudimentary administrative structure and a disciplined army.

47

BUILDING THE NEW STATE

During the thirty years of war that preceded the independence of Eritrea, and particularly during the 1980s, the EPLF leadership started tackling many of the problems of power, authority, and participation that confronted all of the countries in this study. Power, or control over the country, was not a major problem after May 1991. The defeated Mengistu army had abandoned the territory, and there were no other armed movements in Eritrea to claim a piece of the spoils. While the initial phase of the liberation struggle had been one of factional rivalries of Byzantine complexity, by 1981 the EPLF had imposed itself as the only liberation movement with a presence inside the country and, above all, the only one with an army.[29] Furthermore, the EPLF had largely succeeded in becoming a national organization, with some support in the Moslem lowlands as well as in the Christian highlands, where it had originated.

Despite the unchallenged military position of its forces, the new Eritrean government faced security problems: first, there was the danger that the large liberation army, which no longer had a military mission commensurate with its size, would either turn to politics or start preying on the civilian population; second, there was the possibility that the Islamist opposition, which received support from the Sudanese government and could draw on the discontent of Moslems who had supported the EPLF's rivals, would grow, creating a rift within the country and unleashing the forces of sectarian politics.

Consolidating Power

In 1991, Eritrea was estimated to have about 95,000 men and women under arms. The military was well organized and disciplined, although it had the egalitarian structure typical of many liberation armies, with few ranks and little formality. But it was far too large for a country with an estimated population of about three million. Reducing the military ranks was a delicate operation. The fighters had served for years at enormous sacrifice to themselves and their families and were the heroes of the liberation struggle. They could not simply be dismissed, particularly

---

[29] Ruth Iyob, *The Eritrean Struggle for Independence: Domination, Resistance, Nationalism 1941-1993* (Cambridge: Cambridge University Press, 1995).

given the absence of job prospects, the shortage of land, and the recurrent droughts that left most peasants heavily dependent on international food aid for at least a part of their sustenance.

In this area, as in many others, the EPLF proceeded cautiously and with a great deal of pragmatism. Initially, all 95,000 fighters were kept on in the military, working with no pay, but being fed as they had been during the war. About 8,000 of the combatants—those who had been assigned to administrative duties during the war—were moved to positions in the government bureaucracy. They too served without pay. After the country's official independence in 1993, the difficult process of demobilization began in earnest, with 48,000 combatants demobilized in two phases. In 1993-94, the 26,000 cadres who had joined the EPLF after 1990 were let go with a small cash payment and enough food for six months. In the next two years, another 22,000 soldiers—from among those who had joined before 1990—were demobilized, receiving larger payments, based on their number of years of service, as well as a year's worth of food. As a result, by 1995, the military had been reduced to about 40,000 men and women; some 48,000 former combatants had been demobilized, and another 8,000 were working in the civil service. Despite the reduction, the military establishment still remained very large for a small, low-income country.

From the government's point of view, demobilization was a success, allowing the consolidation of a much smaller army with a more hierarchical, traditional command structure. From the point of view of the released combatants, the program was less successful, in that they were provided with only minimal help to reintegrate in civilian life. Most of the demobilization and reintegration effort was financed directly by the government, through a loan obtained from the Eritrean Commercial Bank, because donors were reluctant to finance the process on the government's terms and because the government, in turn, was impatient with the donors' slowness and their cumbersome procedures.

Although the Eritrean government was anxious to keep the military out of politics, it was not willing to relegate it to a purely military role, isolating it in its barracks. Rather, it wanted the military to remain an active participant in the life of the country, helping in particular to rebuild the physical infrastructure and to foster national cohesion. This was in keeping with the experience of the war period, when by necessity the liberation army had done a lot more than fight the Ethiopian soldiers. It had administered liberated areas, provided rudimentary services to the population, kept roads passable, operated mechanical workshops to keep vehicles and weapons functioning. The military had also been an agent of social change, first by bringing together people from all ethnic and religious groups, and second by integrating women in its ranks—a truly revolutionary change by the standards of Eritrean Moslems and Christians alike.

This tradition of political, developmental, and social activism was kept alive after independence with the introduction of compulsory military service for all men and women between the ages of eighteen and forty. The national service consisted of six months of military training and one year of work reconstructing the country's physical infrastructure. Furthermore, by assigning the recruits to units designed to include young men and women from all ethnic and religious groups, the government relied on the national service to weaken ethnic and religious divisions and foster a new national identity.

Politicized Islam was not an immediate security threat but a difficult, long-term problem with the potential to fester and get out of hand. The country's demographic and economic reality, the history of the liberation struggle, and the geopolitics of the area made the possibility of religious conflict very real.

The population of Eritrea was divided almost equally between Christians and Moslems, with the former concentrated in the highlands and the latter in the lowlands along the Sudanese border and the Red Sea. Historically, the close relationship with Ethiopia, particularly during the rule of Haile Selassie (who thought of Ethiopia as a Christian country surrounded by Moslems), put the Christian population in a dominant position. Moreover, while the entire country was extremely poor and underdeveloped, the largely Moslem lowlands were particularly arid and lacking in infrastructure.

The war for independence had also created some tension between Moslems and Christians. The first significant Eritrean nationalist movement, the Eritrean Liberation Front, was organized in the Moslem lowlands and supported by Arab governments. The EPLF, which emerged later, was initially seen as a Christian movement. The struggle for supremacy lasted through the 1970s, but in the end the EPLF succeeded in marginalizing the ELF and in establishing itself as a national movement. The exiled ELF, however, retained a following among Moslem refugees in the camps in the Sudan.

By the time Eritrea became independent, the ELF had also gained the support of the Sudanese government. Dominated by a coalition of military and Islamist elements since a coup d'état in 1989, the Sudanese government was the antithesis of the EPLF, with its Marxist past and its commitment to social reform. Furthermore, the Sudanese government promoted Islamist organizations in the neighboring countries, while the EPLF was sympathetic to the struggle of the southern population against northern domination.

Thus all the conditions necessary to turn Christian-Moslem relations into a major political rift existed in Eritrea, except for one: there was no strong organization inside the country capable of carrying out an Islamist agenda. The EPLF was too strong and commanded too much allegiance everywhere. The Eritrean Islamic Jihad, the major Islamist group that sought to build on the old following of the ELF, remained a divided organization with limited capacity, despite the assistance it received from the Sudan. Nevertheless, the EPLF perceived political Islam as a potential threat, reacted strongly against it, and in so doing risked driving more Moslems in the direction it wished to avoid. In 1995, angered by the Sudanese refusal to curb the Islamic Jihad's cross-border raids, the Eritrean government invited members of the Sudanese opposition to Eritrea and supported the formation of the National Democratic Alliance, a joint front of Sudanese opposition groups, openly providing it with military assistance.

From Power to Authority

By 1991 the EPLF had not only a government-in-waiting but also a state-in-waiting—with an administrative structure, a disciplined army, and a clear sense of what it wanted to accomplish. But the capacity of this state was woefully inadequate to run a country, even one with as small a population as that of Eritrea.

Building an effective governing apparatus and thus turning power into authority became the main concern of the EPLF.

The country's new leaders brought to the task a mindset shaped by thirty years of war and by their previous ideological commitment. Until the late 1980s, the EPLF leadership had been strongly committed to Marxism-Leninism. Like most liberation movements, it believed in the necessity for control and discipline and was committed to the socialist transformation of the country, including the development of a planned, command economy. In the late 1980s, the EPLF was forced by the changing international situation to abandon socialism and to revise its views on economic development. But the basic stance of its leaders, developed over thirty years of war, did not change: they continued to prize efficiency, discipline, and control; to be suspicious of the intentions of donor countries and international organizations; and to trust the Eritreans' ability to get things done on their own. In their quest for independence, the Eritreans received no support or recognition from any of the international organizations or major donors. The Organization of African Unity and the United Nations never recognized the Eritrean demand for self-determination as legitimate; the United States supported the integrity of Ethiopia until the Eritrean victory appeared certain; and even the socialist countries chose Mengistu over the Eritrean nationalists. As a result, the EPLF felt beholden to no one and was not inclined to accept advice and conditionality. It was even willing to refuse foreign assistance unless it was provided on Eritrean terms and for purposes defined by the Eritrean government. It was not for Eritrea to become a "donors' republic" pushed around by international bureaucracies and NGOs with their own agendas. Nor was this just an initial attitude: Eritrea remains as fiercely jealous of its right to make its own decisions as it was at the outset, despite its heavy dependence on the international community for food.

The EPLF's agenda has included two projects since independence: state-building and nation-building—pursued simultaneously and thus influencing each other. The EPLF has sought to design state institutions that will not only improve administrative efficiency but also unite the population for a common purpose. It has not, however, promoted participation by organized interest groups in an open arena. Mobilization, in other words, has taken precedence over democratic participation.

Between 1991 and 1993, Eritrea was not officially an independent country, although the new Ethiopian government made no attempt to administer what remained on paper a region of Ethiopia. In those two years, the EPLF started laying the groundwork for a new political and administrative system, organizing elections for ten provincial legislatures and for local councils. Like the early elections in Uganda, these were loosely organized no-party elections, conducted without benefit of voter registration or formal procedures. The EPLF also started restoring an administrative structure, relying in part on cadres that had acquired some administrative experience in the war zones and continued to serve as unpaid civil servants.[30]

The independence referendum was organized much more formally, although there was no doubt that the vote would be overwhelmingly in favor of independence. Voters were registered, in an operation that also served to carry out a census of the population and to issue new nationality cards, and international observers were invited to monitor the proceedings. As expected, only a small number of people voted against independence.

With independence formally attained, the EPLF set up a transitional government and undertook the writing of a constitution. The transitional government consisted of a National Assembly and a Council of State. The National Assembly comprised the 75 members of the EPLF's Central Committee, 30 delegates from the regional assemblies, and a further 30 citizens chosen by the Central Committee, of whom 10 were women. The 27-member State Council was made up of 17 ministers and 10 regional administrators. There was no real separation of executive and legislative power: Isaias Afwerki was president, chairman of the National Assembly, and chief executive of the Council of State. Nor was there any real separation between party and government structures.

Since then, the government has introduced new reforms to improve efficiency and to pursue its goal of national unity. In 1995, it undertook a drastic reorganization of the civil service,

---

[30] See Fouad Makki, "Nationalism, State Formation and the Public Sphere: Eritrea 1991-96," *Review of African Political Economy*, Vol. 23, 70, December 1996, pp. 475-97.

cutting the number of employees from 30,000 to 20,000. It was a courageous move, typical of the EPLF's ruthless determination to live up to its commitment to efficiency and austerity. The government has also reduced the number of provinces from ten to six—both to minimize administrative costs and to maximize ethnic and religious pluralism within each region in pursuit of its nation-building ideal.

The outcome of these efforts is a government widely considered by observers to be honest and committed to efficiency, but slowed down in the implementation of policies by the shortage of trained personnel. Corruption has been kept to a minimum, and uncovered cases are dealt with swiftly. The Eritrean leadership remains very suspicious of anything that can be construed as external interference. Confident about its past accomplishments, it believes that it knows what the country needs better than international organizations, donor countries, and international or even indigenous NGOs. It discourages coordination among the aid donors, for example, believing that coordination is the job of the government. In other words, the leadership still places a lot of emphasis on discipline and control.

The aid relationship between the government of Eritrea and the foreign donors is revealing of the attitude. Eritrea is poor, and extremely aid-dependent when it comes to food. Nevertheless, the government refuses to bow to donor pressure, even turning down foreign aid when it cannot obtain it on its own terms. It repeatedly stresses, furthermore, that it will only accept foreign assistance for a few years—until the country recovers from the worst consequences of the war—because in the long run foreign assistance is a trap, leaving a country mired in debt.

The tug-of-war between the Eritrean government and the international donors started at independence, and the U.S. Agency for International Development (USAID) was one of the first agencies to experience a clash of outlook and wills with the Eritrean government. Eritrea at that time urgently needed food relief, because a combination of war-caused disruption and drought left about two-thirds of the rural population with a food deficit and only 6 percent capable of producing a surplus.[31]

---

[31] Dan Connell, "Eritrea: A Revolution in Process," *Monthly Review*, Vol. 45, 3, July-August 1993.

Eritrean needs are not limited to emergency food aid. With a per capita GNP estimated at $200 a year and a literacy level of about 20 percent, Eritrea needs assistance in all areas. Nevertheless, the government in early 1992 did not hesitate to suspend negotiations with USAID because the latter tried to make assistance contingent on the implementation of a privatization program that the government found too inflexible and invasive. It is a reflection of the respect that the prickly Eritrean government commands that USAID eventually gave in—as did many other bilateral and multilateral donors over the next several years. The government also has succeeded in convincing the World Bank to fund an ambitious human capacity-building project about which outside experts initially expressed a great deal of skepticism.

The World Bank's experience with Eritrea is typical. In most of the successful aid negotiations, donors have found themselves in the unusual position of having to accede to Eritrea's conditions, rather than vice versa. The Eritrean government does not allow foreign agencies and NGOs to pay salaries above the level of those prevailing in its civil service, for fear that they will entice the best qualified people away from public service—a common problem in highly aid-dependent countries. The government also insists that donors reduce the amount of money spent on baseline studies and evaluations, particularly when carried out by foreign consultants, arguing that such activities only serve to decrease the amount of assistance reaching Eritrea. It also insists that foreign assistance be channeled through government agencies, not through NGOs; to make sure this will happen, it has closed down the offices of international NGOs.

Despite this extraordinarily hard-line position taken by the Eritrean government, aid continues to come. The obvious dedication, honesty, and seriousness of purpose of the Eritrean government has made many donors anxious to continue working in the country. The international community has come to accept from the Eritrean government behavior that would in most countries lead to the termination of aid.

Rebuilding the Economy

The EPLF's economic policy has evolved in the direction of economic liberalization after 1991, but it has retained vast areas of ambiguity. At the heart of the problem is the attitude of the gov-

55

ernment toward the private sector. Although it had rejected its old commitment to Marxism-Leninism, the EPLF leadership at the time of independence espoused a vision of a "planned and regulated" market economy.[32] By 1994, the vision had moved somewhat closer to the prevailing orthodoxy, but the government still foresaw an important role for the state. The centerpiece of its economic strategy, the government stated in its 1994 *Macropolicy* white paper, was "the establishment of an efficient, outward looking, private sector-led market economy, with the government playing a proactive role to stimulate private economic activities."[33] The major components of the government's strategy for rehabilitation, reconstruction, and development must be human capital formation, export-oriented development in both industry and agriculture, infrastructure development to remove bottlenecks, environmental restoration, and promotion of the private sector.

Parts of this program are being implemented. Human capital formation—that is, education and training—has received much government and donor support. The rehabilitation of the infrastructure has priority in deeds as well as words. In this area, too, the Eritrean government has showed its independence—some would say its stubbornness. In an episode invariably cited by donors as most revealing of the Eritreans' attitude, the government rejected an Italian project to rehabilitate the railroad from the port of Massawa to the capital city of Asmara as too expensive, and decided to carry out the project on its own—reconstructing the rail bed with the same labor-intensive technology with which it was built during the colonial period and summoning out of retirement old train engineers to refurbish the engines. The point is not that the Eritrean emergency rehabilitation is a better choice than the donors' high quality project—which this writer is not competent to judge—but that the government is determined to remain the arbiter of what is best for Eritrea.

In other areas, however, the government's commitment to the principles spelled out in the white paper on macroeconomics appears more ambiguous. One such area is government ownership of productive assets. The government retains ownership

---

[32] Ibid., p.7.
[33] The Government of the State of Eritrea, *Macropolicy*, November 1994, p.12.

of all land and grants farmers—notably women as well as men—
lifetime use rights. It is not clear whether this means that the
government is not totally committed to liberalization and to the
development of the private sector, or whether it has decided to
avoid for the time being the controversy that is bound to arise if
it attempts to transform the extraordinarily complex traditional
land tenure systems into freehold ownership.[34]

Questions about the government's economic vision are also
raised by repeated references to a "Singapore model" of development and by the party's growing involvement in business even
as the state is privatizing its own assets.

The Singapore model envisaged by the Eritrean leaders
appears to entail a combination of a highly disciplined, controlled society and a government policy that aims at developing
infrastructure and human resources to such an extent as to make
Eritrea an attractive service center for corporations operating in
the entire region. Whether or not such a plan is even remotely
realistic given Eritrean conditions, by invoking the example of
Singapore, the Eritrean government is signaling that it sees itself
as the guardian of Eritrean society and economy and that it will
continue both to exercise strict political control and to manage
economic development.

The party's role in economic development is puzzling.
During the war years, the EPLF developed a network of war-
related enterprises in the areas it controlled. Working in
makeshift quarters, often underground for protection from
Ethiopian bombs, the party developed the capacity to manufac-
ture weapons and spare parts as well as to repair vehicles and
other equipment. After 1991, these enterprises became part of a
public sector that also included companies nationalized by the
Ethiopian government in 1975 and inherited by Eritrea. In
1994, the EPLF held its third congress and reached two major
decisions. One, to be discussed later, was to disband the EPLF
and to launch in its place a new organization, the People's Front
for Democracy and Justice (PFDJ). The other was the decision to
separate party and government more clearly in preparation for
an eventual transition to multi-party democracy. Part of this

---

[34] Sandra Fullerton Joireman, "The Minefield of Land Reform: Comments on the
Eritrean Land Proclamation," *African Affairs*, Vol. 95, 1996, pp. 269-85.

process was the division of public sector assets between the PFDJ and the government, with the government keeping the properties inherited from the Mengistu government and the PFDJ maintaining control over the enterprises developed by the EPLF during the war. Since the old Eritrean industries and plantations nationalized by the Mengistu government had been largely destroyed during the war, it was the party that kept control over the most important and viable public enterprises, particularly in the realm of transport and mechanical workshops.

Since the 1994 congress, the government has declared its intention to privatize its share of the public sector and has started doing so. The party has argued that it need not sell its assets because they are not parastatals dependent on government subsidies, thus draining public finances, but commercially run, profit-making enterprises that help develop the country and support party activities. Even if these party enterprises avoid turning into typical money-losing parastatals in the future, the growth of this politically protected sector is a potential obstacle to the development of a genuine, autonomous private sector.

The economic rehabilitation of Eritrea has proceeded very slowly, hampered by the scarcity of natural resources and the destruction caused by the long conflict. The level of dependency on imported food has decreased somewhat, but it is still great and unlikely to decrease any time soon. Growth rates have been satisfactory—but mostly as a result of the normalization of life and economic activity deriving from peace rather than of new development. It is thus far too early to reach conclusions about the effectiveness of the development model chosen by the Eritrean leadership. Eritrea remains a very poor country that is still trying to repair war damage and to reach a minimum level of economic sustainability. There is no Eritrean "economic miracle." The country's economic viability is still in doubt. The Singapore model, which would make the country viable by developing a service economy not dependent on natural resources, remains a distant dream.

THE ISSUE OF PARTICIPATION

Eritrean progress in dealing with stability issues, organizing institutions of governance and administration, and rehabilitating the economy has not been matched by progress in opening up avenues for political participation by individuals and groups free to organize and express their views. In Eritrea, "participation" mostly means mobilization—that is, a government-led effort to make citizens aware of the goals the leaders have set for the country and to work to attain them. The freedom to set goals different from the PFDJ and to pursue them through collective efforts does not exist.

There is nothing in the history of the EPLF and indeed of the country to predispose Eritrea to a "democratic transition." The colonial period gave Eritreans experience with the fascist Italian government, not with a democratic one. The ten years of the federation with Ethiopia, during which Eritreans elected their parliament and political parties functioned, were a brief hiatus that ended with the return to a particularly authoritarian Ethiopian administration. The EPLF's own political mindset, developed during years of war, favors control over freedom of choice.

The EPLF and its successor PFDJ profess commitment to democracy, but their definition of the term appears closer to the socialist ideal of a "people's democracy" based on collective social justice than to the Western model of representative democracy based on individual rights. In a 1997 speech considered by Eritrean officials to offer the best explanation of what democracy means, President Isaias denounced the tendency to focus "on the partial attributes and external forms of democracy, rather than on its substantive and comprehensive contents."[35] He argued that a "robust and participatory democratic system" must incorporate principles of economic fairness and equal opportunity, not only political rights and constitutional guarantees. The process of democratization entails first of all broad participation by the people in all areas, including the economy, and the building of institutions and the development of a political culture; and while pluralism is important to democracy, it is a "distorted notion of pluralism" that measures democracy by the number of political parties.

In view of this statement, it is pointless to analyze at length whether the Eritrean government is democratic by the normal

---

[35] "Democracy in Africa: An African View," Address by Isaias Afwerki, President of the State of Eritrea, Wilton Park Conference, West Sussex, September 8, 1997.

standards: it neither is nor wants to be. The more interesting question is whether the Eritrean government is creating areas of openness and participation, as it claims, or whether statements such as Isaias's are simply a smokescreen for a centralized, authoritarian system—a Marxist-Leninist system minus the ideology. It is thus necessary to ask how the view of democracy articulated by the president is translated in practice. Components of that vision can be found in the effort to promote economic growth discussed above, in the participatory approach to writing the new constitution, and in the rejection of a competitive party system in favor of a "movement" system similar to Uganda's.

In 1994, the transitional government formed a constitutional commission. Like Uganda, Eritrea chose to make the writing of the constitution an exercise in popular mobilization and consensus-building. For two years, the forty-two members of the commission toured the country, holding meetings in villages and listening to the population. The content of the constitution was probably not affected by these meetings, which represented mostly an exercise in popular mobilization and political education.[36] The absence of political parties or autonomous organizations of civil society capable of making concerted inputs into the process limited the possibility of a serious debate on the strengths and weaknesses of the constitutional model itself.

The constitution produced by this process is, at face value, strongly democratic, providing protection for civil and political rights. It calls for a unitary rather than a federal system, with a National Assembly elected by universal suffrage and a president elected by the National Assembly from among its members. The president is head of both state and government, as well as commander of the armed forces. The constitution also calls for the independence of the judiciary.

On paper, the constitution thus contains the major abstract provisions necessary to safeguard a democratic system. But the country lacks the political building-blocks for the development of such a system, and the leadership does not appear to be in a hurry to develop them. The draft constitution was approved in March 1997 by a specially elected constitutional assembly. The

---

[36] The head of the Constitutional Commission, Bereket Haile Selassie, admitted in a conversation with the author that he could have written the same constitution in a few days sitting in his study; he thought, however, that the process was extremely important in that it helped educate the population and build a national consensus.

National Assembly was then put in charge of implementing the constitution. To this end, it has appointed a special commission to draft laws on political parties and elections. The process has not yet been completed, and the delay appears to be deliberate.

Even if the formal process is completed and the laws necessary to implement the constitution are enacted, major structural problems are bound to hamper democratization. Political parties, autonomous organizations of civil society, and an independent press always take time to develop. They can be expected to take even longer in Eritrea, even if they are allowed to form, because the PFDJ had both legitimacy and a strong organizational structure.

In 1998, the PFDJ remained the only legal political organization in the country. Self-described variously as a front, a party, or a movement, the PFDJ has all the characteristics of the mass single parties of the early post-independence African period. Membership is open to all, and other mass organizations, such as women's and youth associations, are affiliated with it. It is theoretically distinct from the government, but in reality there is little difference between the two. Government and party officials like to declare their commitment to a democratic system, but they also argue that new parties cannot be conjured into existence to please the donors and will only emerge slowly.

Autonomous organizations of civil society are also absent in Eritrea, and they are not encouraged to form. The leadership does not hide its contempt for the narrow range of donor-dependent organizations often considered to constitute civil society. Eritrean organizations are not allowed to receive foreign funding, except on rare occasions when the government permits them to do so, mostly for the purpose of acquiring specific equipment. The government is determined to remain the only conduit for foreign assistance and to maintain control over all development efforts. An independent press does not exist, although some simple news sheets are beginning to appear, and some Ethiopian publications were distributed in Asmara before hostilities between the two countries started in May 1998.

Nothing summarizes better the conundrum of democracy in Eritrea than the tension between individual rights and the common good embodied in the constitution. The charter protects the normal panoply of individual rights, including the right of free speech and the right to form associations. But the constitution also clearly spells out the duties of citizens, including owing allegiance to Eritrea, completing "one's duty in the national service," and advancing national unity. In the government's interpretation, the enjoyment of rights appears contingent on the fulfillment of duties. In a harsh decision that caused much international criticism, for example, the Eritrean government denied civil rights to all Jehovah's Witnesses because they refused to vote in the referendum on independence and because their sons and daughters refuse to participate in the national service.[37] In the eyes of the government and, it appears, of most Eritreans, Jehovah's Witnesses have declared themselves not to be part of Eritrea and thus forfeited their rights. In the Eritrean system, the collectivity remains much more important than the individual.

CONCLUSIONS

Eritrea shares with Ethiopia and Uganda the central concern with the reconstruction of state and economy as a goal which, in their views, must take precedence over considerations of participation and democracy. But Eritrea has gone a step beyond the other two countries in its single-minded determination to pursue those goals efficiently and quickly. The early experience of Eritrea must be understood by looking not only at the policies but also at the moment: the early post-independence period after a long bitter struggle. This special moment has carried Eritrea successfully through many initial difficult tasks, with the population willing to accept government control without much resentment. But this moment cannot last forever, and the government is bound to confront a more skeptical population within a few years. The outbreak of the border conflict between Ethiopia and Eritrea might postpone that skepticism for a while, but not indefinitely.

The government's concern with development and equity is real, as is its determination to curb corruption and to set an efficient and austere example of how a country should be run. It is

---

[37] Craig Calhoun and Pamela De Largy, "Rights After Liberation," *Dissent*, Vol. 43, 3, Summer 1996, pp. 129-33.

typical of the present Eritrean leadership that it has taken seriously the formation of the office of the Auditor General, which is held in high regard by the donors. Party discipline and genuine commitment have been sufficient initially to prevent the abuses of power usually found in countries where no institutions exist to hold the government accountable. And there is no evidence of gross human rights violations and overt repression. Rather, a war-weary population appears mostly content to get back to a normal life and let the PFDJ run the country.

The government's approach thus has been fairly successful initially. The question is whether the situation can continue, or whether this benevolent, top-down system will soon start degenerating into a malevolent authoritarian one. The key to the answer is probably the success or failure of economic development. Fairly high rates of economic growth might keep a population tired of war and conflict sufficiently satisfied to prevent conflict over multi-party democracy—confirming Isaias's claim that substantive democracy is initially more important than formal pluralism. Economic policy is thus crucial not only to Eritrea's economic future, but to its political future as well. The Eritrean government appears to have chosen the ambitious model of the East Asian developmental state, despite the lack of human resources to bolster it. The leadership is energetic, disciplined, and cohesive, but this may be insufficient.

It is quite clear that foreign donors will have little impact on the evolution of the Eritrean system. The leadership is determined to pursue its own policies in its own fashion, and donor assistance is only accepted if it conforms with the government's plans. Donors can choose to get out of Eritrea or to play the game by the PFDJ rules, but modifying the rules is not an option at this time. Most are choosing to stay and to play by the rules: despite all the doubts that remain about the long-term effect of its policies, the Eritrean leadership has been able to inspire considerable confidence in its ability and determination.

Chapter 5

ETHIOPIA AND THE CHALLENGE OF POLITICIZED ETHNICITY

After the defeat of Mengistu in May 1991, the new government of Ethiopia faced three major problems very similar to those confronted by Uganda and Eritrea: power—how to establish its control over the entire country; authority—how to institutionalize and legitimize that power; and participation—how to open up better channels of communication between the government and the citizens, allowing a degree of popular control over policies and increasing acceptance of the government.

The Ethiopian solutions to these common problems have been shaped by the extreme politicization of ethnicity and by the mindset of the leaders, which combines the old socialist faith in the capacity of the state to direct and even to engineer change with the new-found conviction that socialist solutions have failed and that the energy of the state should be directed to fostering a market economy. This has resulted in a regime that looks to the old Soviet model for an answer on how to handle ethnicity and to Korea and Taiwan for examples of the governed market economy that Ethiopia wants to develop. The combination has produced conflicting forces. The dynamics of the ethnic federation have created the requirement for centralized political control to combat the centrifugal forces of decentralization. The dynamics of growth stimulated by the economic reforms, on the other hand, is becoming a source of pluralism and of pressure on the government to carry out more far-reaching policy reform. While continuing to resist political liberalization, the Ethiopian government is being pushed toward further change by the logic of the economic policies it has chosen.

65

REBUILDING THE STATE

In 1991, the survival of the Ethiopian state was threatened. The struggle against the Mengistu regime had been waged by organizations promoting ethnic nationalism among Ethiopia's diverse population, not by forming a coalition around an alternative political and economic program. As a result, the disintegration of Ethiopia was a real possibility. The independence of Eritrea—a fait accompli, although officially postponed for two years—set an example. The EPLF's argument that Eritrea was a unique case of deferred decolonization, and thus did not create a precedent other regions of Ethiopia were entitled to follow, may have been correct from a strictly legal point of view, but it was irrelevant politically. Indeed, at a conference of Ethiopian organizations held in London in May 1991, when the collapse of the Mengistu regime was imminent, representatives of the Oromo Liberation Front initially sought to distance themselves from the proceedings. They argued that Oromos were not Ethiopians, and therefore should not participate in the setting up of the Ethiopian government but should concentrate instead on organizing their own state of Oromia. This was precisely the position the EPLF was taking. While the OLF eventually backed down from its initial demands and joined the government, its initial stance was a reminder that strong centrifugal forces were at play everywhere, not just in Eritrea. No movement outside Eritrea, however, had the cohesion, leadership structure, and ability to govern a new state. Disintegration in 1991 meant not the division of Ethiopia into a number of new states, but the collapse of central authority followed by chaos.

The first step in rebuilding the state was creating a framework to accommodate politicized ethnicity. In 1991, the TPLF had power based on its military superiority over the other movements. It could not transform such power into political authority without dealing with the ethnic problem. As a Tigrean nationalist movement, it had no support in other regions, nor could it hope to gain it—Oromos and Amharas could never vote for a party dedicated to the cause of Tigrean liberation. In the last period of the war against Mengistu, when the fighting started spreading from Tigray to other regions, the TPLF took the first steps to address the problem, promoting the formation of ethnic movements in other regions and of an umbrella organization, the Ethiopian People's Revolutionary Democratic Front (EPRDF) to bring them together. But in 1991 these EPRDF-aligned parties were perceived as tools of the TPLF and thus had little legitimacy; many of their officials were young draftees in the Mengistu army who had defected or were taken prisoner and had then turned into party organizers with the sponsorship of the TPLF. Furthermore, they were competing with preexisting ethnic movements like the OLF. More drastic measures were needed.

The TPLF found its inspiration in Lenin's approach to "the problem of the nationalities" and in the Soviet model of ethnic federalism. Paradoxically, the system was failing in the Soviet Union just when it was being replicated in Ethiopia. Lenin advocated the right of nationalities to self-determination, even to the point of secession, and so did the Tigreans—first as radical students and later as leaders of the TPLF. Once the TPLF was in power, however, self-determination for all nationalities had little appeal. Having won the war, its leaders were interested in governing the country, not in supervising its dismemberment. Lenin had faced the same problem, and the TPLF adopted his solution: ethnic groups would be given their own states, but the same strong party would be in power everywhere, thus keeping the country together. In the Soviet Union, the Communist Party had played such a unifying role. In Ethiopia, it would be the EPRDF, which brought under one umbrella the ethnic parties that, in the TPLF's plan, would control their respective regions.

The solution chosen for the problem of the nationalities also provided the TPLF with the framework for tackling the problems of security, administration, and, to a much lesser extent, participation. Ethiopia became an ethnic federation, but this allowed little space for democracy; ethnic nationalism and unity could only be reconciled if one party controlled all the regions. Citizens in the various regions could not be allowed to vote for any party of their choosing lest the country be dismantled.

Consolidating Power

The lingering problem of security in Ethiopia was mostly the result of ethnic conflict. The Mengistu army suffered too complete a defeat to continue resistance in any form. With its command sapped by repeated political purges since the late 1980s, most of its soldiers demoralized, and unmotivated draftees press-ganged to fight for a cause they did not support, it stopped fighting even before Mengistu fled into exile to Zimbabwe in early 1991. The TPLF army marched into Addis Ababa without encountering significant resistance.

Demobilizing the Mengistu army of 500,000 thus proved remarkably easy politically, although it represented a major logistical undertaking that taxed the new government's limited capacity. With financial support from the international community, but mostly relying on its own resources for management, the new government succeeded in demobilizing the entire army by the end of 1991. Soldiers were encamped, registered, given a brief orientation on issues of political reconciliation, and taken back to their villages—or, if they wanted, to urban centers. Food was provided for a period, and in rural areas some received an ox each and agricultural implements. It was not a model demobilization program by international standards, but it was quick, in line with the country's financial and organizational capacity, and it worked.

The much smaller militias of other armed ethnic liberation movements were a more serious threat to stability, because they were still willing to fight and indeed were encouraged to do so by the success of the TPLF. The OLF, whose small force of a few thousand had mushroomed to more than 20,000 men in the first few months after the fall of Mengistu, was the most significant threat to the new government, which responded with a mixture of political and military means.

The OLF was a weak organization, but it could claim to represent about 40 percent of the population, and it thus resented the dominant position that the TPLF enjoyed after the fall of Mengistu. Faction-ridden, poorly led, and chronically unable to decide whether its ultimate goal was an independent Oromia or a federal Ethiopia, it had been an ineffective participant in the war against Mengistu, doing little fighting. Although it could claim to represent only 10 percent of the population, the TPLF was both politically and militarily a far stronger movement. Making things more complicated, the OLF was loosely allied with the TPLF during the war, but never became part of the EPRDF, which included instead a rival organization, the Oromo People's Democratic Organization (OPDO).

The TPLF first attempted to work out a political solution. In July 1991, a meeting of all political parties—almost all ethnically based—was held in Addis Ababa to set up a transitional government. The EPRDF-affiliated parties received 32 of the 87 seats in the Council of Representatives set up at the conference, while only 12 went to the OLF. Since the remaining seats were divided among more than twenty small parties, the EPRDF and the OLF dominated the Council—but the EPRDF could always outvote the OLF. The meeting also adopted a Transitional Charter and agreed to a complex transition process, which would start with local and regional elections, followed by elections for a constituent assembly, the adoption of a constitution, and finally parliamentary elections. The agreement also called for the encampment of the OLF's militia and of a portion of the TPLF's army.

Because neither side was committed to the compromise, the agreement was short-lived. On the eve of the June 1992 local and regional elections, the OLF, justifiably convinced that there was no possibility of a fair contest, ordered its militia to decamp and pulled out of the elections. Other parties not affiliated with the EPRDF also withdrew.

From that point on, the TPLF dealt with the OLF as a security problem to be solved by force. The TPLF army enjoyed overwhelming superiority, and the war did not last long. By late summer, 18,000 OLF fighters had been taken prisoner; they were demobilized and later freed. This short conflict eliminated the major domestic security threat faced by the government, but it also narrowed its political base, reducing participation and increasing control. The OLF itself was reduced to an ineffective organization without a strategy to re-engage politically and without the capacity to bring about change by force.

Establishing Authority

In May 1991, the major Ethiopian political organizations were divided about the future of the country—about whether it should continue to exist and, if so, in what form. At one extreme, the anti-EPRDF All-Amhara People's Organization (AAPO) was a firm believer in a united Greater Ethiopia and even refused to accept the inevitability of Eritrean independence—it had been

69

an Amhara emperor, Menelik, who had expanded the boundaries of Ethiopia to where they are now, and another Amhara
emperor, Haile Selassie, who had governed Greater Ethiopia for
the next half a century. At the other extreme, the OLF wavered
between the ideal of an independent Oromia, the desire for a
large degree of autonomy, and the dream of supplanting the
TPLF as the dominant political organization in the country. The
TPLF remained convinced that a united Ethiopia could only survive as a federation of ethnic states. Since the TPLF had power,
its solution prevailed.

The Transitional Charter adopted at the Addis Ababa conference in July provided the first outline of the ethnic federation.
It proclaimed the right of all "Nations, Nationalities and
Peoples"—the difference was not clearly defined—to self-determination, meaning each had "the right to administer its own
affairs within its own defined territory."[38] Under the Charter,
however, ultimate power resided with the central government.
This consisted of a council of representatives and an executive
comprising a president, a prime minister, and a council of ministers. All positions in the transitional government were alloca-
ted by negotiations among the parties participating in the meeting, with the EPRDF affiliates constituting the largest bloc in
both the council of representatives and the cabinet, but with
other parties, particularly the OLF, also represented. While ultimately the power of the transitional government resided in the
uncontested military control of the TPLF army, the Addis Ababa
meeting represented an attempt to build a more inclusive political base.

A few weeks later, the government issued a proclamation
that divided the country into twelve ethnic regions and two
autonomous cities, giving them, at least on paper, substantial
administrative and fiscal powers. It was clear, however, that the
new regions were subordinate to the authority of the central government.

The establishment of the regions sharpened the political
differences between the EPRDF and the autonomous ethnic parties and also increased ethnic tensions in rural areas. Inevitably,
the AAPO was incensed by what it considered to be the dismem-

---

[38] Fasil Nahum, *Constitution for a Nation of Nations* (Lawrenceville, N.J.: Red Sea Press, 1997), p. 39.

berment of Greater Ethiopia, while the OLF thought the charter and the proclamation did not give sufficient powers to the regions. Less noticed was the stirring of ethnic conflict in rural areas, with episodes of "ethnic cleansing" of minorities from regions that were not theirs. Amharas were the most frequent targets in these incidents, because many had been settled by the emperor in the newly annexed areas or had been placed there as administrators in order to strengthen central control and were thus resented by the local population.

In 1994, Ethiopia adopted a new constitution. From a preamble stating "We the Nations, Nationalities and Peoples of Ethiopia" to the provisions spelling out the procedures to be followed by a nation wanting to secede or one wanting to form its own state within the federation, the document confirmed the centrality of ethnicity to the new political system. The fourteen regions were replaced by nine states (the city of Addis Ababa retained special status), which were granted extensive powers spelled out in the constitution and all residual powers not explicitly reserved for the federal government.

All available evidence suggests that the government has made serious efforts to transform Ethiopia into a federation by building up the capacity of the states to carry out their functions. These efforts have received considerable support by foreign donors favoring decentralization, and this provides some independent evaluation of the progress of the new federal system. A team fielded by the Harvard Institute for International Development, which in late 1995 undertook a project to help the government strengthen its budget and financial planning system, concluded that the government had a real commitment to devolution, above all in the field of finance and budgeting, with regional officers beginning to develop their own policies and systems different from those at the center.[39] While the tax base of the state governments remains narrow, necessitating transfers from the central government, these transfers are increasingly in the form of bloc grants, which allow the states to make autonomous policy decisions. The 1996-97 budget shows that, out of a

---

[39] This section is based in part on personal communications with John Cohen of the Harvard Institute for International Development. See also his earlier studies on this issue published by the Institute (HIID, Cambridge, Mass.): "Transition Toward Democracy and Governance in Post-Mengistu Ethiopia," Development Discussion Paper No. 493, June 1994; and "'Ethnic Federalism' in Ethiopia," Development Discussion Paper No. 519, October 1995.

total federal budget of Birr 9.5 billion, Birr 3.3 billion were subsidies paid to the state governments and controlled by them.[40]
These and other changes suggest that a transition toward federalism is taking place on the ground, not only in words. With the
federal government raising about 85 percent of domestic revenue
and receiving all foreign assistance, the states still have little financial autonomy. However, the most important states—particularly
Amhara, Oromia, and Tigray—are beginning to cover much
higher percentages of their budgets from their own resources.

Efforts are also under way to build up the administrative
capacity of the states. A civil service college was set up to train
state and local administrators, and many foreign donors are
engaged in capacity-building programs ranging from training
personnel to the provision of computers. Local governments,
particularly at the district level, also receive serious attention.
The efforts testify to the government's will to organize an effective, decentralized system and to the donors' support for the
project. Progress is slow, because of the initial weakness of all
local and regional government institutions. Nevertheless, federalism is becoming a reality.

Politically, however, there is no decentralization. EPRDF
affiliates dominate all the regions, thus guaranteeing the basic
homogeneity of policies. With the backing of the TPLF and the
EPRDF, access to greater resources, and strong-arm methods
that make it difficult for opposition parties to compete, the
EPRDF affiliates control, in the words of an Ethiopian official,
"most of the political space," leaving the opposition to operate
at the margins. Faced with the certainty of defeat, most opposition parties, including the OLF, choose to boycott elections, thus
surrendering the political space even more completely to the
government parties.

Reforming the Economy

The Mengistu period was one of economic deterioration. After a
promising beginning with the implementation of a long overdue
land reform, the socialist government imposed increasingly centralized control over all aspects of economic activity, and particularly over agriculture, the sector from which almost 90 percent

---

[40] Economist Intelligence Unit (EIU), "Ethiopia," EIU Country Profiles and Reports,
December 10, 1997.

of Ethiopians derive their livelihood. The potential benefits of freeing the country from land tenure systems that most experts considered to be a hindrance to rural development were never realized because the government imposed even worse obstacles in the form of collectivization. The war further weakened the economy by causing destruction of infrastructure, disrupting normal activities, and taking half a million men away from their fields and into the army.

The TPLF thus inherited a moribund economy. Jettisoning its old Marxist-Leninist ideological cargo, the Meles regime embraced the challenge of economic liberalization and restructuring more vigorously than most African governments. Three aspects of the economic policy in Ethiopia are worth mentioning: the first is the serious commitment to economic liberalization, coupled, as in Eritrea, with the government's determination to continue to guide economic development, or to "govern the market" like Korea and Taiwan; the second is the decision to maintain all land in the hands of the government; and the third is the continuing role of the party in the economy, particularly in Tigray. There are thus some considerable similarities in the way Ethiopia and Eritrea approach economic reform. The outcome, however, is different: presiding over a much larger, diverse, and complex country, the TPLF does not have the same degree of control as the EPLF. As a result, the private sector is beginning to have a greater impact on economic policy.

In early 1992, the transitional government embarked on a standard program of macroeconomic reform. In January, the World Bank extended a $657-million economic recovery and reconstruction loan. In the next few years, the Ethiopian government devalued the currency, reduced the fiscal deficit, curbed inflation, eliminated price controls at the retail level, liberalized imports, and abolished government monopolies in domestic marketing and exports—in other words, it started implementing a structural adjustment program. At the same time, it took the first steps to attract new investment through a reform of the investment code, and to strengthen the private sector by privatizing parastatals.

The commitment to reform has won the Ethiopian government continuing high levels of assistance from the World Bank, support from bilateral donors, an IMF Enhanced Structural

Adjustment Facility loan, and debt rescheduling by the Paris Club of major lending nations. The outcome of these basic reforms has been positive, with GDP growth rates increasing to more than 5 percent a year in the late 1990s. The dependence of the Ethiopian economy on agriculture, however, and thus its vulnerability to drought, is revealed in the swings of GDP growth. From a high growth rate of 12 percent in 1993, when the rains were good, GDP growth declined to 1.7 percent in 1994 because of drought.[41]

Although it has abandoned the notion of economic planning and recognized a need for liberalization, the government has not accepted a completely free-market approach. Having systematically studied the experience of other developing economies, particularly of the more successful East Asian countries, the government has come to the conclusion that Korea and Taiwan offer the model that Ethiopia should try to replicate. Ethiopian officials refer to this model as the "governed market" (an expression borrowed from Robert Wade's 1990 book, *Governing the Market*, a study of economic policy in Taiwan). They argue that the experience of the socialist countries shows the failure of government as entrepreneur, but that the experience of Taiwan and Korea suggests that the highest growth rates are achieved by countries where the government does not take a hands-off approach to economic development but, by providing incentives, coaxes private investment to serve an overall strategy. In the case of Ethiopia, the overall strategy must be "agricultural development–led industrialization": growth in agricultural production must be promoted to make the country self-sufficient in food and to increase rural incomes sufficiently to create a market for consumer goods, which in turn will support the development of small and medium-size processing industries. As part of this strategy, the government has restructured public expenditure, reducing the allocation for defense while almost doubling expenditure for health and education and more than quadrupling expenditure on roads, particularly in rural areas. With the support of donors, and working with state and local

---

[41] Economist Intelligence Unit (EIU), "Ethiopia," op. cit.; and World Bank, Population and Human Resources Division, Eastern Africa Department, Africa Region, "The Federal Democratic Republic of Ethiopia: Ethiopian Social Rehabilitation and Development Fund Project," March 13, 1996, pp.1-2.

governments, the Meles regime has also sought to provide funding for locally initiated development projects funded in part by the communities themselves. While these efforts help meet only a small part of the country's social and economic needs, they denote a commitment to rural development. At the same time, the government has also started looking beyond the basic strategy, seeking ways to accelerate the pace of industrialization by creating incentives for exporters.

This development strategy has evolved gradually. There appears to have been much discussion within the TPLF leadership and much fear initially of loosening government control excessively. Privatization has proceeded slowly, and until early 1998 the government insisted both that telecommunications and electric power production should remain a government monopoly, and that foreign banks should not be allowed to operate—at least not until indigenous banks had been established and the government had strengthened its capacity to regulate the banking industry. The investment code was initially also quite restrictive. But economic policy continues to evolve, partly as a result of an intellectual process and partly as a pragmatic response to pressures. For example, after accepting the concept of the governed market, the government has become more willing to privatize remaining state enterprises and more sensitive to the requirements of the private sector. The investment code has been amended repeatedly; telecommunications and electric power generation have been opened to private investment; and there is widespread expectation that the government will be forced to allow foreign banks to operate in Ethiopia lest economic growth be stifled by the shortage of credit.

The government has, however, drawn the line at the privatization of land, which was first nationalized by the Mengistu regime in 1975. Multilateral and bilateral donors do not like the decision, although many acknowledge that privatizing land would be an enormously difficult undertaking fraught with economic, political, and social tensions. Privatizing land is not simply a question of reversing Mengistu's nationalization decree. Such a move would only reinstate the tangle of feudal and communal land tenure systems that were considered an obstacle to economic growth in the early 1970s. The transition to a freehold land tenure system, on the other hand, is bound to be a lengthy and above all conflictual process. As in Eritrea, the government has decided to postpone facing the problem.

The role of the TPLF—and to a lesser extent that of other EPRDF-affiliated parties—in the economy is another unresolved and controversial issue lending a degree of ambiguity to Ethiopia's economic reforms. The economic role of the political parties is easier to explain in terms of its historical origin than as part of a governed market model of development. During the war years, the TPLF, like the EPLF, started developing a public sector in the areas it controlled. This public sector included assets controlled by so-called NGOs, of which the most important was REST (Relief Society of Tigray). REST was formed in the late 1970s to facilitate food distribution to areas affected by drought and war—the policy of the TPLF was to convince foreign donors to provide assistance directly through REST, rather than through the Mengistu government, implicitly giving recognition to the TPLF institutions while depriving the Ethiopian government of a source of patronage. REST was fairly successful in attracting donor support. In the process, it also acquired assets such as trucks and repair facilities that allowed it to transport and distribute relief goods. Toward the end of the war, the TPLF also launched the Tigrean Development Association, a development NGO, in order to attract further international support for development projects. Since 1991, the TPLF's involvement in the economy has increased further—through a network of supposedly private corporations controlled by prominent TPLF officials and believed to have been funded by the party.

The TPLF's involvement in economic activity was formalized in 1995 with the creation of the Endowment Fund for the Rehabilitation of Tigray. The Fund controls non-military assets captured from the old regime, companies established by the TPLF during the war, funds provided by the party, funds received from international NGOs, and even capital borrowed from the state-owned Commercial Bank of Ethiopia. Alone or in joint ventures with private companies, the TPLF has launched a considerable array of projects, which, it claims, are run as commercial enterprises, not as subsidized parastatals.

This pattern of economic entrepreneurship by political organizations is replicated in other regions, particularly the more developed ones, although on a much smaller scale. In the absence of good information—studies are incomplete and based on hearsay as much as on hard data—it is difficult to evaluate the actual size of this sector or its long-term importance. Some analysts see the party enterprises as a residue of previous policies that is certain to diminish in importance as the economy grows and a genuine private sector develops. Others see it as an obstacle to economic growth, believing that the party-linked enterprises will never function along purely commercial lines, and that they will push genuine private entrepreneurs out of the most promising areas by getting better access to credit and licenses.[42]

In the reconstruction of the Ethiopian state, economic restructuring appears to play a particularly important part—much more so, probably, than in Eritrea or in Uganda. In all three countries, of course, the revival of economic activity is essential not only to improve people's lives but also to provide the government with the funds necessary to maintain stability, to strengthen government institutions, and to supply basic services to the population. In the case of Ethiopia, however, the economy also appears to provide the most important area of openness and pressure for further change, forcing the government to re-evaluate its policies. To the extent that a glimmer of pluralism can be detected in Ethiopia, it is the result of increased private sector economic activity.

THE ISSUE OF DEMOCRACY

Among the three countries discussed, Ethiopia is unique in having formally embraced the principle of multi-party democracy, holding local and regional elections in 1992, elections for a constituent assembly in 1994, and parliamentary elections in 1995. It is also the country with the least popular participation in any form. The initial weakness of the new government's position in most parts of the country and the strength of politicized ethnicity explain the paradox of democratic form without democratic content.

The political, as opposed to military, control of the TPLF was extremely weak in 1992. For most Ethiopians, it was an alien

---

[42] See John Young, "Development and Change in Post-Revolution Tigray," *Journal of Modern African Studies*, Vol. 35, 1, 1997, pp. 81-99.

movement. For years it had fought a ruthless battle to keep other political organizations out of Tigray—for example, destroying the Ethiopian People's Revolutionary Party, whose members had sought to regroup in the mountains of Tigray after being driven out of Addis Ababa by Mengistu's forces, rather than cooperating with it against the common adversary. Until about 1990, the TPLF also presented a forbidding ideological facade, with an uncompromising dedication to a Stalinist interpretation of Marxism-Leninism that led its leaders at one point to proclaim themselves "pro-Albanian." The TPLF thus isolated itself both through its ethnic exclusiveness and its extreme ideological stance. The development of ethnic parties affiliated with the EPRDF was designed to overcome this isolation but proved inadequate.

Political weakness and ideological inclination made the TPLF an unlikely movement to embrace multi-party democracy, but it was given no choice. The TPLF—having been helped by the United States to enter Addis Ababa without encountering resistance (Assistant Secretary of State for Africa Herman Cohen was instrumental in negotiating the agreement that spared the city the final battle)—could not ignore U.S. pressure, and the United States and other members of the international community wanted multi-party elections. Democracy promotion was in its infancy at the time, and it is doubtful that much thought was given by anybody to the question of what the real impact of elections in Ethiopia might be under the prevailing circumstances. Donors instead focused on the principle, demanding elections from the new regime as a demonstration of good will. Neither Museveni in Uganda nor Isaias in Eritrea came under such pressure initially—Museveni because he came to power before multi-party elections had become the litmus test of a government's international acceptability and Isaias because EPLF control over the country was so complete that even enthusiastic supporters of forced democratization saw it was futile to talk of elections.

In reality, elections were futile in Ethiopia as well. The militarily strong TPLF was politically weak, and the opposition parties were even weaker. Forced to accept multi-party elections in 1992, the TPLF made sure that the EPRDF affiliates won everywhere. Indeed, in most districts only EPRDF affiliates participated, either because other parties were not allowed to register their candidates under various pretexts, or because they withdrew from the elections at the last minute.[43] The 1994 and 1995 elections were less chaotic but hardly more democratic, since the only significant opposition parties did not participate.

Despite all the elections, Ethiopian citizens have had fewer opportunities to exercise choices than those of Uganda and even of Eritrea. The formal model based on party competition has failed, and there have been few other outlets for participation. The drafting of the constitution was accompanied by a process of popular consultation, but it was not as extensive as in Uganda and Eritrea. NGOs are allowed to carry out relief and development activities, but they are closely monitored, and projects that can be construed as political are banned. In any case, the domestic NGO sector in Ethiopia is considered to be in its infancy even by its members. International NGOs seeking to promote democracy and human rights are also closely monitored. Independent publications are allowed, but editors and writers are subject to frequent imprisonment and harassment—particularly those writing for the virulently hostile Amhara publications that the government accuses of fomenting ethnic hatred.

There is a partial exception to this picture in Tigray. During the war years, the TPLF, initially a movement of urban intellectuals, had to reach out to the peasants and to mobilize their support. In the areas where it achieved control, it did so in part by responding to peasant demands for education, land redistribution, better local administration, and fairer courts. Within the limits of its capacity it established elected local councils, opened schools, and organized mass associations—but it also expected peasants to put in long days of unpaid labor on rural development projects such as terracing hillsides against soil erosion, or building microdams for irrigation and domestic water consumption. The result was a mixture of mobilization, coercion, and genuine participation—including endless sessions of criticism and evaluation. It was this type of participation—within the strict framework provided by the party—that constituted the TPLF's idea of democracy.[44]

---

[43] *An Evaluation of the June 21, 1992, Elections in Ethiopia* (Washington, D.C.: National Democratic Institute for International Affairs and the African American Institute, 1992).
[44] John Young, *Peasant Revolution in Ethiopia* (Cambridge: Cambridge University Press, 1997), Chapter 7.

In an interview granted to a Tigrinya-language publication in 1997, Prime Minister Meles Zenawi elaborated on the TPLF's concept of democracy.[45] Democracy, Meles declared, "is the participation of the people of a country in issues that they believe in." The greatest democracy "is the participation of the people at the grass roots level." This is not the democracy expected by the United States, he added, because that country lacks broad participation by the people.

Extending the TPLF's concept of democracy to the entire country has proven very difficult; more important, studies conducted in the mid-1990s suggest that even in Tigray the system is eroding. Like many other revolutionary movements, the TPLF is discovering that it is difficult to sustain high levels of mobilization once peace has returned. Since the end of the war, peasants in Tigray have become less willing to provide free labor and more inclined to demand government help. The population of the towns, which remained under the control of the Mengistu government until the end, is not willing to accept regimentation. And the endless sessions of self-evaluation are proving incompatible with the normal functioning of the economy and administration.[46]

With the revolutionary democracy of the war years eroding and the formal democracy promoted by the donors remaining a fiction, there is not much room for participation in Ethiopia in the late 1990s. The best hopes in this direction appear to be the progress of decentralization and the strengthening of local government, as well as the continued evolution of economic policy that has enhanced the influence of economic interest groups. But this is a slow process, and in the meantime the authoritarian features of the regime are evident. The annual human rights reports on Ethiopia by the U.S. Department of State—and particularly the lengthy report issued in 1997 by Human Rights Watch—provide accounts of numerous violations.[47]

---

[45] The interview appeared in *Hiwyet*, No. 11, May 1997. The discussion here is based on an unofficial English translation provided by the Embassy of Ethiopia in Washington.
[46] John Young, "Development and Change in Post-Revolutionary Tigray," op. cit.
[47] U.S. Department of State Bureau of Democracy, Human Rights and Labor, "Ethiopia Country Report on Human Rights Practices," various annual issues; and Human Rights Watch, "Ethiopia: The Curtailment of Human Rights," *Report*, Vol. 9, 8 (A), December 1997.

CONCLUSIONS

The centrality of politicized ethnicity has made the Ethiopian case the most politically complex of the three transitions being considered. Neither the reconstruction of the state and the economy nor the opening of institutions to greater popular participation could proceed without a mechanism for dealing with politicized ethnicity. Certainly the Ethiopian government thought this was the case. In the already-mentioned interview, Meles argued that democracy has two preconditions: the presence of a government that discourages the supremacy of one nationality, and the creation of a collective identity. There was no strong collective identity in Ethiopia in 1991, at least not among members of the political elite, and there is no indication that such a common identity is emerging now. As for the government's commitment to the equality of all nationalities, the TPLF portrays the ethnic federation as a sign of that commitment, while its opponents claim that the federation is simply a divide-and-rule device to ensure Tigrean domination.[48]

The possibility of Ethiopia's emerging as a democratic country in the future depends ultimately on whether ethnic federalism evolves in the direction of a genuinely decentralized system, giving all groups an incentive to remain part of Ethiopia. The answer is not yet clear. The TPLF is giving every sign of wanting to remain in control, but it cannot do so without devolving power to the ethnic states. If the states become reasonably successful in providing good administration, and if the country continues to experience some economic growth, few Ethiopians (even in the political class) will continue to see the federation as an instrument of domination, and political liberalization may take place without leading to the disintegration of the country. If the economy stagnates, the states fail to develop the capacity to formulate their own policies, and the population remains deeply dissatisfied, ethnic nationalism is unlikely to be contained by the federal solution, and the government will turn to repression in order to prevent the disintegration of the country.

In the aftermath of the May 1991 takeover, the international community—especially the United States—tried to pro-

---

[48] John Young, "Ethnicity and Power in Ethiopia," *Review of African Political Economy*, Vol. 23, December 1996, pp. 531-42.

mote a swift democratic transition in Ethiopia. The attempt was particularly clumsy. The demobilization of the OLF militia and the development of a national army were not undertaken at all; the technical preparations for the elections were rudimentary; political preparations were non-existent. No steps were taken to level the playing field even a little. No attempt was made to develop minimal consensus about the post-elections policies among the parties.[49] The elections, in other words, were poorly prepared.

The real problem, however, was much deeper: Ethiopia was no longer a unitary state, but it had not become an ethnic federation. With the state itself still being contested, it was impossible to make it democratic. Furthermore, the economy, characterized by a large subsistence peasant sector and a small state-controlled industrial and service sector, did not easily provide the underpinning for a pluralistic system.

The situation has evolved considerably since 1992, with the ethnic federation becoming a reality and economic growth providing the basis for the formation, in a rudimentary form, of diversified interest groups not dependent on the state. But the changes are only beginning, and the obstacles to a positive outcome remain considerable. The states are starting from an extremely low point in terms of their administrative capacity and their resource base. The economy is growing rapidly, with Addis Ababa seemingly a boom town in the late 1990s, but poor infrastructure, shortage of credit, weak legal frameworks—all the evils afflicting countries in the early stages of economic reform—remain a threat to continued growth. The transition is bound to remain slow and complex.

---

[49] See John Harbeson, "Elections and Democratization in Post-Mengistu Ethiopia," in Krishna Kumar, ed., *Post-Conflict Elections, Democratization and Democratic Assistance* (Boulder, Colo.: Lynne Rienner, 1998), pp. 111-32.

Chapter 6

FOLLOWING THE EXAMPLE? RWANDA AND THE DEMOCRATIC REPUBLIC OF THE CONGO

Discussions of the new African leaders have suffered from a great deal of confusion about who should be included under that rubric. There is no doubt that Museveni, Meles, and Isaias constitute the core of the group. But the outer boundaries are uncertain, with some commentators extending them to embrace anybody who has come to power in recent years. Such broad definitions are not very useful. What sets apart the leaders discussed in this study is the policies they have embraced, not the date of their accession to power or their age. Their distinctive approach to the reconstruction of the state and its transformation, which calls into question the adequacy of the model favored by the donor community, is what makes them worth discussing.

Paul Kagame of Rwanda and Laurent Kabila of the Democratic Republic of the Congo have often been included in discussions of the new leaders. The inclusion is understandable. Paul Kagame is extremely close to Museveni and was supported by him in the effort to build a liberation army and to launch the struggle against the incumbent regime in Rwanda. Together, and with some support from Isaias and Meles, Museveni and Kagame also helped Kabila in his fight against Mobutu. The policies pursued by Kagame show many similarities to those followed by the other new leaders. Kabila talked the same language for a while, although he never really implemented the policies. In fact, by the summer of 1998, Kabila had become the enemy of Museveni and Kagame, who, disillusioned with his policies and his incapacity to control the eastern Congo, threw their support behind his opponents.

Rwanda and the Democratic Republic of the Congo (DRC, formerly Zaire) have been much less successful in addressing the challenges of power, authority, and participation than have Uganda, Eritrea, and Ethiopia. Despite the vigorous attempts by the Rwandan Patriotic Front and Paul Kagame, Rwanda—following the genocidal massacres of 1994, the continuing tensions between a predominantly Tutsi government and extremist Hutu militias, and the reciprocal fears of Hutus and Tutsis—is still teetering on the edge of chaos. The Congo, under the mediocre leadership of President Laurent Kabila, flounders on with no apparent plan for state consolidation.

The two countries are worth considering, however, because they call attention to important issues involved in the reconstruction and eventual democratization of African states. Most importantly, the experience of Rwanda brings into sharp focus the conundrum of politicized ethnicity and its impact on state reconstruction and democracy, thus complementing the discussion of Ethiopia. The case of the DRC, on the other hand, helps underline the differences between the politics of the new leaders and the politics of the old African elites epitomized by Mobutu and, it seems increasingly evident, Kabila as well.

RWANDA

The central problem for Rwanda in the entire post-independence period has been that of ethnicity, or the difficult relationship between the Tutsi minority and the Hutu majority. Scholars debate whether Hutus and Tutsis are really different ethnic groups, or simply occupational castes that the colonial powers misrepresented as "tribes" because it suited them to do so. In terms of today's politics, the debate is irrelevant, and the answer is clear: Hutus and Tutsis have come to see themselves not only as distinct ethnic groups, but as enemies. No amount of historical and anthropological analysis can define that problem out of existence:

> Increasingly in the post-independence era, the terms [Hutu and Tutsi] have assumed additional meanings, which refer to the atrocities that have been carried out in both Rwanda and Burundi. Thus, in one sense, being a Rwandan Tutsi today means belonging to the community whose families

have been persecuted since 1959, and who were slaughtered in the genocide of 1994. To be a Rwandan Hutu is to be part of the community that was massacred in Burundi in 1972, 1988, 1990 and 1991, and that has members in exile in the Democratic Republic of the Congo or Tanzania.[50]

Hutus dominated the politics of Rwanda after independence. In 1990, however, the Rwandan Patriotic Front (RPF), a Tutsi insurgent group organized among refugees in Uganda, invaded Rwanda and eventually seized control of some areas in the north of the country, causing the flight of about a million Hutus. An RPF attempt to march on Kigali in 1993 was halted by the Hutu government of President Juvenal Habyarimana with the help of the French. At a meeting held in Arusha, Tanzania, in August 1993, regional leaders succeeded in mediating a compromise between the government and the RPF. Under the terms of the agreement, the two sides agreed to cooperate in a transitional government of national unity and to form a new national army integrating elements from the government Forces Armées Rwandaises (FAR) and the Rwandan Patriotic Army (RPA).

The accord triggered much opposition among Hutu extremists, resulting in the marginalization of moderates and the increasing prominence of hard-liners in the government. The final blow in an increasingly unstable situation was the shooting down of the plane in which President Habyarimana was returning to Kigali from a regional meeting in April 1994. The downing of the plane was never adequately explained, but there is no doubt about what happened next. Hutu extremists took over and immediately launched a genocidal campaign to exterminate Tutsis. In response, the RPF resumed its campaign and marched into Kigali in July. The RPA commander, Paul Kagame, emerged as the dominant figure in the regime, officially occupying the positions of vice president and minister of defense.

By the time the RPF established its control over the country, at least 800,000 Rwandans, mostly Tutsi but also Hutu moderates, had been slaughtered in a systematic campaign spearheaded by the extremist Hutu militia, known as the

---

[50] Economist Intelligence Unit (EIU), "Rwanda," EIU Country Profiles and Reports, September 19, 1997.

Interahamwe, while hundreds of thousands of refugees had streamed across the borders into Tanzania, Burundi, and above all Zaire. The advance of the RPF also caused the perpetrators of genocide, fearful of being caught in a wave of retribution, to follow the refugees into exile. When the situation stabilized, seething camps in eastern Zaire housed a mass of one and a half million people, including not only bona fide refugees but also members of the Interahamwe and the FAR that had perpetrated the genocide. Perhaps another half a million refugees had found their way into Burundi and Tanzania.

The Problem of Security

By the late summer, the RPF controlled Rwanda, but it still faced a major security problem. Driven from the country, elements of the Interahamwe and the FAR were regrouping and re-arming in the refugee camps, and they soon started launching cross-border raids into Rwanda. With the international community willing to address the refugees' physical needs but not the political crisis that was developing in the camps, the armed groups established their rule, controlling access to food and shelter and preventing the refugees from going back to Rwanda, where stability was returning; the militias needed the real refugees to remain in the camps in order to keep international aid flowing. Despite repeated warnings by human rights organizations about the situation in the camps, the international community refused to commit the resources needed to separate the refugees from the rearming genocide perpetrators and to bring the latter to justice.

But the government of Rwanda could not ignore the situation. Cross-border raids were increasing in number and severity, raising the possibility of a more massive onslaught in the future. After warning the international community repeatedly that it would be forced to take matters into its own hands if the situation was allowed to continue, the RPF government in late 1996 helped organize and arm an anti-Mobutu group, Alliance des Forces Démocratiques pour la Libération du Congo-Zaire (AFDL), which drew much of its support from the Rwandan minority in eastern Zaire. With the active support of Rwandan troops, the AFDL attacked the refugee camps and broke them up. The Interahamwe thus lost its grip on the refugee population, and 1.2 million people returned to Rwanda, the majority of them in a matter of days. The AFDL, under the leadershij Laurent Kabila, eventually went on to overthrow Mobutu Sese Seko and to establish a new government in Zaire (subsequent developments in Zaire will be discussed below).

Initially, the breakup of the refugee camps put an end to the cross-border raids, improving security in Rwanda, but the respite was short-lived. First, a considerable number of armed Hutus crossed back into Rwanda with the refugees. Although the government tried to screen and disarm the returnees, their number was so overwhelming and their return so sudden that many armed men who in all probability had taken part in the genocide managed to get through. Their return created pervasive insecurity and fear within the villages as returning *génocidaires* sought to eliminate potential witnesses to their crimes and as survivors sought revenge. Secondly, other elements of the Interahamwe and the FAR managed to regroup on the Zairian side of the border, resuming cross-border raids. RPA troops trying to stop these incursions used a heavy hand against civilians suspected of helping the rebels, thus further alienating the Hutu population, already worried that the new government was dominated by Tutsis. As mentioned earlier, the attacks by the Interahamwe also caused instability in western Uganda.

The lack of security remains a dominant problem in Rwanda. In contrast with Uganda, where insecurity is limited to specific areas, the problem in Rwanda is pervasive, providing the background against which all reconstruction efforts take place. The possibility of new mass violence hangs over the country.

Reconstructing State and Society

The Rwandan government faces the task of reconstructing not just the state but the society as well. Conflict has deeply affected social life in all of the countries considered in this study, but nowhere has it become so intimately part of social relations, pitting neighbors against each other, as in Rwanda. There is no spatial separation between the ethnic groups, whose members historically live intermingled house-by-house in the same villages. The legacy of communal violence is particularly extensive and brutal. Finally, the country has experienced a demographic change that almost defies understanding.

87

Before the 1994 genocide, the population of Rwanda was 7.6 million. Of this total, at least 800,000 and possibly one million people were killed, and some two million became refugees in neighboring countries. Then, after the RPF came to power, some 700,000 of the 1973 Tutsi refugees returned from Uganda, and in 1996 at least 1.2 million of the 1994 refugees also came back from Zaire. More refugees came back in the following months. As a result of these movements, the population of Rwanda in the late 1990s is still about 7.6 million people. They are not, however, the same people. The country faces a problem of social reconstruction for which there is no model because there is no precedent.

Rwanda has started nevertheless to take some steps toward the administrative and economic reconstruction of the state, following a model that appears to owe much to Museveni's. This is not surprising. The RPF and its leadership came from the Tutsi refugee community in Uganda. Many of the fighters, including Paul Kagame, gained their military experience fighting in Museveni's National Resistance Army. Relations between Kagame and Museveni remain close.

Government. Establishing a system of government in Rwanda means moving from the power of an essentially Tutsi (hence minority) military movement to the authority of national institutions. The RPF has taken some steps to make the government more national and some to make it more institutionalized.

It has sought to make the regime more national and broad-based by reaching informal agreements with other political parties and implementing the power-sharing clauses of the Arusha agreement—it was opposition to this agreement that led Hutu extremists in the former government to instigate the genocide in an attempt to halt the process. Although political organizations other than the RPF remain officially suspended, individuals belonging to pre-1994 political parties have been incorporated in the cabinet, and seats in the National Assembly and control over local government are also shared with them. In late 1997, members of the RPF only controlled six of seventeen ministries in addition to the presidency. As the only legal political organization and the one that controls the army, however, the RPF maintains political control. Excluded from power-sharing, not surprisingly, are the two Hutu extremist parties most responsible for the genocide.

The constitution, rewritten in 1995, calls for a multi-party system and also incorporates the Arusha accord of 1993, and thus the principle of power-sharing. Nevertheless, the government has made no move to legalize the activities of political parties; nor has there been serious discussion of organizing elections. With the memory of the massacres fresh in everyone's mind, even the international community is in no hurry to push Rwandans to the polls, fearing an ethnic vote that would reignite conflict. While the rejection of elections is both an understandable and probably the only realistic course of action in Rwanda, it also makes it difficult for the government to acquire a more national character and greater legitimacy.

Among the consequences of the genocide has been the weakening of all the country's institutions as trained cadres were killed or fled. Reviving institutions in these circumstances is extremely difficult, but some change is taking place. The National Assembly is trying to carve out a role for itself, although it remains a weak component of the political system. Within the executive, the role of the presidency has also become somewhat more limited, although less by institutional design than because Paul Kagame concentrates so much power in his own hands—in early 1998, he added the chairmanship of the RPF to his other positions.

The institutions that may be most crucial in determining whether Rwanda will avoid another catastrophe in the future are the judiciary and the local governments, both woefully inadequate. There are over 100,000 people jailed in dramatically overcrowded prisons, awaiting trial as suspected *génocidaires*. Somehow, they have to be brought to justice, because a failure to do so could incite extremism on both sides: among Tutsis seeking revenge, and among Hutus seeking to forestall such revenge and to regain the upper hand. The collapse of the judiciary, however, has resulted in excruciatingly slow processing of the extraordinarily large number of cases, with consequently long pre-trial detention periods and lack of expertise in the conduct of the trials. While the government appears to be committed to trying the prisoners, instead of executing them summarily in revenge (as it would have been all too easy to do after the mass slaughter of 1994), its capacity to do so—and with full respect of the law—is extremely limited.[51]

Local government remains an even more problematic area. With tensions between ethnic groups high in every village, Rwanda needs effective local government that the population can trust. It needs local institutions to help bring about reconciliation and to give people a sense of security. But there is no such system of local government. Plans to restructure local administration remain murky, with some talk of regrouping the population into new villages. The military continues to be a pervasive presence—inevitably, given the security situation, but nevertheless to the detriment of civilian authority. Strengthening local government is made even more complicated by the presence of a large number of international NGOs that play an important and useful role in distributing food to returning refugees, rebuilding houses, and in general tending to the needs of displaced people, but that at the same time undermine local government by taking over some of its functions. The weakness of local government contributes to the fragility of peace and security in Rwanda.

Economic Reconstruction. Economic reconstruction has been relatively successful. The country's gross domestic product (GDP), after undergoing a sudden decline in 1994, has grown at an impressive rate of 24 percent in 1995 and 13 percent in 1996. Although these figures reflect recovery from collapse rather than new growth, recovery is important in itself, since it means the country's economic life is returning to normal rather quickly despite the massive population turnover.

But normal is not good enough. Rwanda is an overpopulated country in a generally underpopulated continent. With one of the lowest urbanization rates in Africa, it is also an agricultural country in which land is increasingly scarce. The shortage of land causes economic hardship and also increases political tension, fueling competition. Pressure on the land is made more acute by the fact that agriculture not only has to feed the population but also provides the country's only sources of export revenue: tea and coffee.

---

[51] See Samantha Power, "Life after Death," *New Republic*, April 6, 1998.

The RPF government's economic management has been adequate. The lack of resources, however, has prevented the high rate of economic growth that might alleviate political tension. The government has not been able to restore its tax collection capacity or to control spending and inflation. It has shown commitment to liberalization by allowing the currency to float, reducing tariffs, and allowing repatriation of profits by expatriates. It has reduced the size of its civil service, a process facilitated by the flight of most civil servants in 1994, and it has demobilized some 5,000 of its former total of 20,000 troops. Rwanda thus falls in the same pattern as the other three countries discussed here in its commitment to streamlining government expenditure and liberalizing the economy. Political instability and demographic pressure, however, remain major obstacles to a real reconstruction of state and society—and even more so to any form of political participation and democracy.

The Issue of Participation

In less than four years in power, starting from complete collapse and in the face of a continuing lack of security, the RPF has probably gone as far as it could in reconstituting a government apparatus. But it has not even broached the issue of popular participation, in part because participation on the basis of majoritarianism would again put the Tutsis in jeopardy. The ethnic imbalance, with Hutus accounting for about 85 percent of the population, makes any process of popular consultation explosive in the absence of reconciliation or of a viable framework for coexistence and power-sharing.

What can bring about reconciliation after genocide is a question nobody can answer at this point, because there is no comparable situation. Trying the suspected *génocidaires* in a timely and fair manner might help, but the weakness of the judiciary is an obstacle that cannot be easily remedied. Organizing a process similar to that of the South African Truth and Reconciliation Commission, or similar organizations in other countries, might also help. And the experience of Mozambique suggests that traditional rituals of repentance and atonement can be surprisingly effective in surmounting obstacles to reconciliation in the villages. All this, however, must be considered speculation at this point, because no other country has ever faced a situation where the number of victims constituted such a high percentage of the population.

Devising a framework for power-sharing among Hutus and Tutsis is also a particularly difficult task, as the violence that followed attempts to implement the Arusha accord shows. The obstacles to devising a workable framework are many. A framework that disregards ethnicity cannot work, because the issue is so highly politicized. One based on proportional representation for the two groups in all institutions would leave the Tutsis too vulnerable. A solution based on regional autonomy, as in Ethiopia, is not possible, because there is no physical separation of the two groups. A strong system of local government might help by allowing communities to deal with their problems as they see fit, but local government is no substitute for a national government. The answer remains elusive, and thus Rwanda is a long way from solving the problem of participation.

THE DEMOCRATIC REPUBLIC OF THE CONGO

The characteristics of the new leaders and of the political and economic model they are promoting becomes clearer by looking at President Laurent Kabila and the Democratic Republic of the Congo. Although Kabila owes his position to the support he originally received from Kagame and Museveni, and to a lesser extent from Isaias and Meles, he belongs to a different world in his economic as well as political thinking. He has failed to make progress in solving any of the problems confronting his country and has alienated his former supporters; as of the end of 1998, both Uganda and Rwanda have thrown their support behind a new rebel movement trying to overthrow him, and war is again raging in the country.

Kabila's outlook was shaped in the 1960s and does not appear to have changed. A supporter of Patrice Lumumba in the early days of Congolese independence, he held out in the mountains along the country's eastern border ever since Mobutu's rise to power—a petty warlord surviving on smuggling and, in one case, the kidnapping for ransom of four American researchers engaged in the study of mountain gorillas. In his early days, he developed a grudge toward the United Nations, whose intervention in the Congo in the early 1960s he saw as an anti-Lumumba operation rather than a peacekeeping one. He is still suspicious of the United Nations and of the international community in general, and he appears incapable of dealing with it effectively. Like the new leaders, he does not believe in formal multi-party democracy, but, in contrast with them, he has failed to broaden his power base and to open up some space for participation in other forms. Finally, there is little indication that he understands the realities of the international economy in the 1990s, or that he is able to capitalize on the country's natural wealth in order to attract the investment it needs.

That Kabila should have started with the ideas of the 1960s is not surprising: he spent decades in isolation before being plucked from obscurity by regional leaders seeking a way to make eastern Zaire unsafe for their enemies. But Kabila's ideas have not evolved noticeably since he came to power and faced the challenge of governing a state in the late 1990s. Museveni, Isaias, and Meles have been able to throw off much of the baggage of their original intellectual formation, to learn from the experience of past African failures, to adopt programs of economic reform that win them the praise of the international community, and to seek ways to broaden support for their regimes by opening some avenues of participation. Kabila, like Mobutu, has no discernible game plan other than to stay in power. He has mismanaged major economic issues, making questionable deals with multinational corporations interested in exploiting the Congo's mineral wealth and unmaking them in equally questionable fashion—not a way to attract serious investors. Politically, he has also behaved erratically, antagonizing domestic constituencies and the international community alike, seemingly for no particular reason.

Laurent Kabila appeared suddenly on the political scene in October 1996 as the spokesman for the Alliance des Forces Démocratiques de Libération du Congo-Zaire (AFDL), at the time a somewhat nebulous coalition of Mobutu's opponents. Central to the coalition were the Banyamulenge, Tutsis who had been living in eastern Zaire for hundreds of years but who had been increasingly marginalized by the Zairian government since the crisis in Rwanda. An expulsion order against the Banyamulenge in South Kivu in early October provided the catalyst for an eight-month process that started with the formation of the AFDL and culminated with the flight of President Mobutu

Sese Seko from Zaire and the AFDL's entry into Kinshasa in May 1997.

The fall of the Mobutu regime was brought about more by its own weakness than by the strength of the AFDL, and this explains many of the subsequent problems. In 1996, Mobutu was already at the end of his life, both physically and politically. Seriously ill with advanced prostate cancer, he was losing the capacity to outmaneuver all adversaries that had kept him in power for thirty years. The countries that had supported him during the Cold War—the United States, France, and Belgium—no longer viewed him as the key to Zaire's stability. The economy, run into the ground after decades of mismanagement, had long ceased to provide reliable revenue to the state's coffers. More recently, it had no longer even provided constant infusions of money into Mobutu's own purse, thus decreasing his room for political maneuver. The vast Zairian army was unpaid, demoralized, and undisciplined; even the allegiance of the elite units on which Mobutu relied was in doubt at the end.

The AFDL itself was not a strong organization with much internal coherence. From the beginning, it was a coalition of internal Zairian groups and troops from Rwanda and Uganda. Because of the rapid advance of its forces, which met with little resistance from Mobutu's army, the AFDL did not have the time to consolidate into a coherent organization. If anything, success made it an even more motley coalition, for it picked up other supporters and other agendas as it went along. Internally, provincial governors, opposition political parties, and organizations of civil society started looking at the AFDL as a means for getting rid of Mobutu at last. Externally, the MPLA government in Angola (whose major opponent Jonas Savimbi was supported by Mobutu) got into the fray, helping bring back the Katangese gendarmes and even supplying its own troops[52]; more support came from Eritrea and Ethiopia, which had no direct interest at stake but identified with the revolt against Mobutu. It would have taken an extremely capable leader to give a sense of direction to such an incoherent organization. Kabila was not such a

---

[52] The Katangese gendarmes were the remnants of the army of secessionist Katanga (now Shaba province), who fled into exile in Angola after the collapse of the secessionist government in the turbulent early years of independence in the Congo. The Katangese gendarmes—and their descendants—were supported by the MPLA government as a potential anti-Mobutu force.

leader, as became increasingly clear after the fall of Mobutu removed the enemy that had brought all groups together. The internal coalition disintegrated, and external supporters started questioning Kabila's competence, eventually turning against him.

Reconstructing the State

Once Kabila marched into Kinshasa, he confronted the same basic problems as the other new leaders: restoring security, rebuilding the state, and reviving the economy. He tackled each of them badly. As for the problem of establishing some form of participation, he did not even try, and there is no indication that he saw this as a necessary step. The most notable aspect of Kabila's efforts was the seeming absence of a plan or a concept of how to reconstruct the state. In this climate of uncertainty and lack of guidance from the center, a new armed opposition group arose, seeking to overthrow Kabila, while the eastern Congo turned again into an uncontrolled frontier territory where the Interahamwe could reorganize and other armed groups could operate. Just over a year after coming to power, Kabila faced an armed opposition supported by Rwanda and Uganda, which again felt threatened by attacks coming from the Congo. (This renewed conflict will be discussed in the next chapter.)

Power. Kabila has not succeeded in consolidating his power. Security has remained the major challenge for the DRC all along. The most visible and urgent problem has been the presence of a considerable number of armed groups in the eastern Congo: opponents of the Rwandan and Ugandan regimes, opponents of Mobutu, and eventually opponents of Kabila. Furthermore, the remnants of Mobutu's army, the Forces Armées Zairoises (FAZ), remain a threat, not as a coherent anti-Kabila army, but as armed groups ready to lend their services to anyone who will pay them.

Kabila, however, has confronted a more fundamental problem: the danger that any attempt to restore the state, imposing central authority on a country that has been largely ungoverned for many years under Mobutu, will cause a strong reaction—and, in some provinces, possibly secessionism.

Even after the dismantling of the refugee camps, the DRC's eastern border has remained an area of great instability, with an ever-changing kaleidoscope of political movements forming, disbanding, and reassembling in new formations. In broad outline, the area is contested territory between the Banyamulenge and other ethnic groups; it harbors the remains of the Interahamwe and the FAR, as well as other groups opposed to the governments of Rwanda, Burundi, and Uganda—with a sprinkling of Congolese organizations with unclear agendas and changing alignments, such as the MaiMai.[53] This lawless region also harbors the new anti-Kabila forces.

The army of the Democratic Republic of the Congo is not up to the challenge of maintaining security in this complex area. After the fall of Mobutu, the AFDL was reorganized into the Forces Armées Congolaises (FAC), widely perceived in the country to be dominated first by Rwandan and then by Congolese Tutsis. While this was true initially, the situation became more complicated as Kabila tried to reduce his dependence on a single group. Thus, while Tutsis continued to dominate the FAC in the eastern border area for months, the Katangese presence became strong in Shaba. Furthermore, soldiers of Mobutu's army were also integrated into the FAC. The new army has thus been plagued by a lack of cohesion. Different groups of soldiers have even been paid, at least in theory, according to different scales; in reality, the bankrupt DRC government has found it as difficult to pay soldiers and civil servants regularly as had Mobutu.[54] Far from beginning to consolidate into a more homogeneous force, the FAC is undergoing a new crisis as Tutsis have turned from Kabila's major allies into his bitter enemies.

Paradoxically, the weakness that has made it difficult for the government to effectively control the eastern border region has reduced the probability of attempted secessions. Except in the early days of independence, when Katanga (now Shaba) declared itself independent under the leadership of Moise Tshombe, there have been no threats to the country's territorial integrity. At the same time, however, Zaire has not really been governed as one country. For twenty years, the mismanaged state has been unable to provide even the most basic administration and services. By default, the provinces have gained considerable autonomy—as shown, for example, by the variety of currencies in use in the country: in 1998, Kasai was still using the old Zaire

---

[53] A good summary is provided in *Africa Confidential*, Vol. 39, 4, February 20, 1998.
[54] Ibid.

banknotes, although they had been officially discontinued in 1993; in Shaba, the one million New Zaire notes were legal tender, but they were not accepted in Kinshasa.[55]

The de facto autonomy of the provinces has been gained without an open challenge to the central state; rather, it emerged from a vacuum of power. Attempts to strengthen the central government and to restore a nationwide system of administration will challenge the power of the provinces. Restoring the Congolese state will require either a process of negotiation between the central government and the regional authorities, which Kabila does not appear inclined to undertake, or a process of repression, which the AFDL and later the FAC are not equipped to carry out. The weakness of the Kabila regime reduces the possibility of a confrontation between the central government and the provinces, but it leaves the state in its long-standing condition of collapse.

Government. Kabila has made little progress in the political and administrative reconstruction of Zaire. His main political concern has been to eliminate adversaries and to protect his position. He appears to have no plan for dealing with ethnicity, the de facto autonomy of the provinces, other political parties, or organizations of civil society—or for re-establishing a system of local government. Rather, he has handled problems piecemeal and increasingly with repression. Political parties have been banned, but they are allowed to continue informally, and their leaders are not targets of government repression. Organizations of civil society and independent media are harassed. Nevertheless, Kabila claims that multi-party elections will be held in 1999. To that end, in October 1997 he even set up a constitutional commission of eleven hand-picked historic personalities and twenty-five experts to draft a constitution by March 1998. The constitution was then to be taken to the regions for public discussion, before being approved by an appointed Constituent Assembly and then submitted to a referendum. Although the constitutional commission produced a draft of the document on time, the process had no credibility inside or outside the country and ground to a halt as war resumed.

---

[55] "Democratic Republic of the Congo," in *Africa Review* (Essex, England: World of Information, 1998).

The absence of a workable plan has not only been a problem of the first few months, which could have been understandable for a government that came to power so swiftly. The problem has persisted and indeed worsened as Kabila has started to rely on the tactics of his predecessor—co-opting some potential adversaries, imprisoning others, and playing one person against another in order to stay in power. Increasingly, it has been "Mobutuism Without Mobutu."[56]

Any attempt to reconstruct the state would require considerable international support, given the destruction of both the administrative and physical infrastructure. But Kabila has not been able to convince the international community of his ability as a leader and of his commitment to bring about real reform in the country; as a result, he has received little assistance.

The major point of friction between Kabila and the donors has been his handling of the U.N. investigation into alleged mass killings of Hutu refugees by the AFDL or by Rwandan troops. As already mentioned, after the dismantling of the refugee camps in eastern Zaire, the majority of the refugees and even many of the *génocidaires* returned to Rwanda. But some—possibly as many as 200,000 to 300,000—fled west, deeper into Zaire, and for a while disappeared entirely. Eventually, many reappeared and were repatriated. Some of the ex-FAR and Interahamwe members became soldiers of fortune, reappearing in other conflicts in the region, for example in the Congo (Brazzaville) in late 1997. But some were never accounted for, and it was rumored that large numbers were massacred. The international community, still trying to atone for the failure to stop genocide in Rwanda, responded by calling for an investigation almost as soon as Kabila gained control of Kinshasa. Efforts to send in a U.N. team to investigate the alleged massacres came to naught. Kabila promised cooperation, then denied the U.N. team access to the region, then changed his mind again and allowed the investigation to resume, only to throw new obstacles in the way of its work. After months of wrangling and futile efforts, the investigation was finally called off by the United Nations.

---

[56] *U.S. News and World Report*, November 24, 1997.

The Economy. Economic rehabilitation has also proceeded very slowly. Although a year after the takeover there were some signs of progress in the development of a plan, the renewed fighting has dashed any hope of implementation. The first statements on the economy issued by the Kabila government were confusing, with a mixture of socialist rhetoric, acknowledgment that the market needed to play an important role, and calls for foreign investment. In reality, Kabila has continued to follow Mobutu's example of financing his government at the expense of sustained economic growth. Even before his victory, he was working out ad hoc deals with foreign corporations interested in the country's mineral wealth in order to get quick cash for the AFDL. In at least one case, however, he later reneged on the deal: in January 1998, he canceled a contract for the exploitation of the Kolwezi copper mine granted earlier to American Mineral Fields and instead signed a new contract with a consortium of several companies.[57]

Parallel to these non-transparent deals, however, technocrats in the government have also been trying to draft a more systematic reconstruction plan, which was first presented to an informal group of potential international donors—the Friends of the Congo—at a meeting in December 1997. The Economic Stabilization and Reconstruction Program (ESRP) called for the investment of $1.6 billion for the 1998-99 period—about $400 million from the government's budget, $500 million from the international community, and the rest from the private sector. The plan has not received the necessary financing, largely because donors have been unwilling to make a substantial commitment until the government's human rights and democratization record improves. Without such assistance, however, a credible stabilization plan cannot be put in place, decreasing the chances that the private sector will step forward with large investments. Without stabilization and investment, however, the government does not have the revenue to finance its share of the reconstruction plan or to reconstruct a system of government.

---

[57] Economist Intelligence Unit, "Democratic Republic of the Congo," EIU Country Profiles and Reports, February 10, 1998; Carole Collins, "Reconstructing the Congo," *Review of African Political Economy*, Vol. 24, 74, December 1997; and "Democratic Republic of the Congo," *Africa Review*, op. cit.

At the heart of this vicious circle is Kabila's lack of leadership and of a vision for the Congo. Leadership and a firm vision have allowed Museveni, Isaias, and Meles to move forward, to gain some international support, and to be given the benefit of the doubt. Under Kabila, the DRC is stagnating with no obvious way forward.

CONCLUSIONS

Rwanda and the Democratic Republic of the Congo continue to face critical situations, but for very different reasons. The government of Rwanda appears to have a vision and a plan for political reorganization and economic reconstruction, with strong similarities to those of the countries discussed earlier, particularly Uganda. The ethnic problem faced by Rwanda, however, is so extreme that it defies solution and risks derailing all other efforts. An Ethiopian-style ethnic federalism is not the answer for Rwanda, because of the intermingling of Hutus and Tutsis in all villages. An Eritrean-style attempt to forge a common identity cannot succeed after thirty years of conflict culminating in the deaths of 800,000 people and the displacement of millions. A Ugandan-style reliance on local-level participation in a no-party system also offers no solution, because conflict permeates every village in the country. Vision and leadership are not enough to lift Rwanda out of crisis and to put it on the way to recovery.

The government of the DRC faces many problems, but not seemingly insurmountable ones. The destruction of the country's physical and economic infrastructure, the demoralization and corruption of the political class, and the deterioration of the economy are major problems. But the social fabric has not been destroyed, and people can live with each other fairly peacefully in most of the country. Furthermore, the size of the Congo, its great mineral wealth, and its importance to the stability of the entire region guarantee that international support and foreign investment will be available to help in the reconstruction of the country. What is missing more than anything else is leadership—both to negotiate political solutions among domestic actors and to give confidence to external actors that aid will not be wasted and that investment will pay off.

Chapter 7

GOING BEYOND THE BORDERS

The controversy surrounding U.S. policy toward the new leaders is based not only on their lack of democracy, but also on their aggressive foreign policies. The two are closely related, part of the same attempt by the new leaders to reconstruct their states and make them viable. Domestically, as the previous discussion shows, the leaders are seeking to turn collapsed or new states into well-functioning countries following their own approach rather than the paradigm of democratization offered by the donors. In their foreign policies, they are confronting the regional conflicts that affect their countries. If they deem it necessary, they are even going against well-established international principles and the positions defended by the Organization of African Unity.

The assertiveness of the new leaders' foreign policies is understandable, given the number of cross-border conflicts affecting their countries and the incapacity of international or regional organizations to deal with them. The dangers these countries face are not imagined. The chaos in the eastern Congo is a real threat for Rwanda and Uganda, and the Islamist regime in the Sudan is a threat to all its neighbors. It is hardly surprising that assertive leaders do not remain passive in the face of such threats. But the new leaders' assertiveness across borders is only a short step from aggression, and their unwillingness to continue accepting international policies that they regard as failed is only a short step from disregarding international norms altogether. The dangers of this assertiveness and defiance of norms became most evident during 1998, when a border conflict unexpectedly erupted between Ethiopia and Eritrea, and again when intervention by Uganda and Rwanda in support of anti-

Kabila rebels compelled Angola, Zimbabwe, Namibia, and Chad to support Kabila.

Three factors help explain the foreign policies of Ethiopia, Eritrea, and Uganda—as well as of Rwanda (in its foreign relations at least, Rwanda must be considered part of this group). The first, discussed earlier, is the recent history of the countries and the personal experience of their leaders that war can put an end to conflicts that diplomacy fails to solve. The second is the failure of African and international organizations to address the conflicts of the region. The third is the depth of the crises engulfing the area, in particular the long chain of interrelated conflicts that sends shock waves from the Horn of Africa all the way across the continent to the Congo (Brazzaville) and Angola. This chain of conflicts is changing the political geography of Africa, bringing together regions with distinct histories (the Horn of Africa, the Great Lakes region, and Central Africa) into a continuous and troubled entity.

The four regimes are the product of war; in all four cases, diplomacy failed to provide solutions. The conflict in Eritrea led to repeated rounds of internal negotiations and external mediation, all of which failed. To a lesser extent, so did those in Ethiopia and Uganda. In Rwanda, international mediation resulted in the 1993 compromise Arusha agreement, but when the implementation failed and genocide ensued, the killing was brought to an end by the advance of the Rwandan Patriotic Army, not by international diplomacy or international intervention. The lesson of the 1994 Rwandan debacle for the four governments is that they cannot rely on outsiders to provide solutions but have to take matters into their own hands.

THE FAILURE OF INTERNATIONAL INSTITUTIONS

International institutions have not served the region under discussion well in recent years—indeed, since the first decade of African independence. The United Nations, the Organization of African Unity (OAU), the major powers, and, increasingly, humanitarian and human rights NGOs have been unable to deal effectively with the conflicts racking the area. This explains—it is a different matter whether it also justifies—the new leaders' contempt for such organizations and propensity to seek their own solutions in defiance of international opinion.

102

The Organization of African Unity (OAU), formed in the early, heady days of African independence when Pan-Africanism was a cherished ideology, has remained in practice a weak organization incapable of playing a major role in preventing or mediating African conflicts. The OAU had two major goals at the outset: decolonization, which included the end of apartheid, and the unification of Africa. But decolonization has now been achieved, and African unity is a forgotten dream. The challenge faced by Africa is to put an end to the violent strife that afflicts many countries domestically and creates tensions among them internationally. The OAU is poorly equipped for this challenge.

In dealing with African conflicts, the organization is guided by two principles, non-interference in the internal affairs of member countries and respect for colonial borders. These principles are both a help and a hindrance in managing African conflicts. Respect for colonial borders undoubtedly has helped maintain peace in Africa. Virtually every border on the continent could be disputed because it is poorly demarcated, because it cuts across old political or ethnic entities, or because it is a remnant of the colonialism whose imposed order Africans have rejected in their struggles for independence. The decision to accept colonial boundaries undoubtedly has spared Africa much strife between countries. Adherence to the principle, however, has left the OAU unable to play a meaningful role once conflicts involving boundaries have erupted. In the thirty-year conflict between the Ethiopian government and the Eritrean nationalists, in the crisis between the Biafran secessionists and the government of Nigeria, or in the war between Ethiopia and Somalia on control over the Ogaden region, the OAU has been bound by its rules to proclaim the sanctity of the status quo even when the status quo guaranteed the continuation of conflict. Eritreans, for example, feel they have been victimized by the OAU's defense of the status quo, and they are as a result utterly contemptuous of the organization.

Similarly, the principle of non-interference in the domestic affairs of member states has made the OAU an ineffective organization. The newly independent African countries, jealous of their prerogatives and unsure of their real strength, have carried the principle of non-interference to an extreme, accepting all African governments, no matter how much they violated internationally recognized principles or how brutally they trampled on the rights of their populations. The OAU has thus turned into an old boys' club of leaders who are not accountable to their populations and who do not hold each other accountable to meet even minimal standards of behavior. A broad church indeed, the OAU has embraced dictators, strongmen, and military leaders without asking questions.

The weakness of the OAU has become particularly clear during the 1990s, when the phenomenon of what has been called the collapsed states acquired great saliency in Africa. In the early 1990s, Somalia, Liberia, and Sierra Leone virtually ceased functioning as states, as the power of armed factions and local warlords overwhelmed that of their governments. Later, Rwanda, Burundi, and Zaire came close to sinking into the same status. As conflict has engulfed these countries virtually without governments, the OAU has not been able to do anything.

The United Nations has had a long and complex relationship with Africa. On security issues, it has often been seen as a tool of the Western powers that dominate the Security Council—Laurent Kabila still so perceives it because of the role the United Nations played in the Congo in the 1960s. Some U.N. agencies, for example the U.N. Conference on Trade and Development (UNCTAD), did serve as arenas in which African and Third World countries could make their voices heard, but in the 1990s, the United Nations has become a symbol of the industrialized countries' indifference, particularly after the tragic events of Somalia made the major powers extremely leery of involvement in new quagmires. As war-triggered humanitarian disasters have multiplied—in Liberia, Sierra Leone, Rwanda, and Burundi—the United Nations and the major powers have sat on the sidelines or, as in Rwanda in 1994, withdrawn when they were most needed. The impression left by these failures is much stronger than that left by the successes that the United Nations achieved in Africa in this period—in supervising the transition to independence in Namibia, for example, or the elections in Mozambique in 1994. Africans have ceased looking to the United Nations to solve their problems.

The new international actors of the 1990s in Africa are the human rights NGOs, such as Amnesty International or Human Rights Watch. Relations between these organizations and many

African governments have soured very quickly. Committed to high principles, and unwilling to make allowances for context, international human rights NGOs have been extremely critical of almost all African governments. This has caused considerable resentment among African leaders, who see such criticism as oblivious to context or, worse, as interference in their affairs, or an imposition of alien standards on Africa. African human rights NGOs, often supported by international organizations and cooperating with them in the monitoring of human rights violations, are perceived by many governments simply as opposition groups funded by foreigners. The new leaders in particular have come to see most human rights organizations as hypocritical and destructive—blindly applying principles to situations they do not understand and doing nothing to help.

The swath of Africa extending from Somalia to Angola and the DRC has been particularly affected by the failure of international organizations. International intervention in Somalia saved lives but failed to restore a viable government. In the Sudan, most international organizations have studiously ignored the conflict that reignited in 1983 and continues unabated fifteen years later. In Burundi and Rwanda, a symbolic U.N. presence has had no impact on the situation, while humanitarian organizations have helped care for the victims, but, overwhelmed with the task, have also ended up by providing food and shelter to the perpetrators of the massacres. In West Africa, Liberia and Sierra Leone have sunken into chaos without an effective response by international organizations.

The perceived failure of the international system has left African countries to deal with problems as best they could. Unlike the international community, or even the OAU, African countries cannot ignore the conflicts in their respective regions, because these spill across borders. As a result, a variety of regional organizations originally created for purposes other than international security and conflict resolution have stepped into the vacuum. In West Africa, the Economic Community of West African States (ECOWAS), an organization designed to promote increased regional trade and economic integration, ended up creating a military force (ECOMOG—the ECOWAS Monitoring Group) to intervene militarily in Liberia and Sierra Leone. And in the Horn of Africa and Great Lakes regions, the

Intergovernmental Agency for Drought and Development (later the Intergovernmental Agency for Development, or IGAD)—an obscure agency formed to provide early warning of drought and locust invasions—has taken it upon itself to mediate conflicts, particularly in the Sudan. But these organizations are themselves weak. In particular, when the multiple conflicts of the Horn and Great Lakes regions started interconnecting, no agency was capable of responding. The new leaders' policies need to be understood against this background of OAU and U.N. ineffectiveness, the unwillingness of the major international players to become involved in conflicts that do not affect their security interests, and the absence of sufficiently strong alternative multilateral organizations.

THE CHAIN OF CRISES

In the early 1990s, a chain of conflicts started developing across Africa, in a wide swath stretching diagonally from the Sudan and Ethiopia in the northeast to Angola in the southwest. This chain includes the Sudan, Eritrea, Ethiopia, Somalia, Uganda, Rwanda, Burundi, Zaire, the Congo, and Angola as the most involved countries, with some others affected to a much lesser degree. While Uganda, Eritrea, and Ethiopia have become much more peaceful internally than they were during the past twenty years, they are today surrounded by deeply unstable countries whose conflicts interlink.

Interestingly, this is not a part of Africa that constitutes a historical unit—as seen by the fact that there is no geographical name to designate all the countries just listed. Ethiopia, Eritrea, Somalia, and the Sudan were traditionally considered part of the Horn; Uganda, of East Africa; Zaire, of Central Africa; and Rwanda and Burundi, of the Great Lakes region; while Angola belonged to Southern Africa. As the importance of colonial ties and of Cold War divisions has receded, the countries have found themselves increasingly linked by new factors. A major such factor—and one that explains how the chain has come to extend across the continent—is the commonality of views and the solidarity that developed among Ethiopia, Eritrea, Uganda, and Rwanda (at least until Ethiopia and Eritrea turned against each other in a border conflict).

Somalia plays a marginal role in this chain of conflict. Ethiopia is the only country significantly touched by events in Somalia, although it is probably less affected by a collapsed Somali state, whose clans are intent on fighting each other, than it was in the past, when a united Somali government claimed the Ogaden region of Ethiopia as its own and waged war to seize it.

The Sudan, on the other hand, is a main link in the chain. The long-standing conflict between the Sudan's Arab north and the African south, never completely settled, flared up again in the early 1980s and became particularly intense after 1989, when a military coup d'état resulted in the formation of an Islamist government led by Lt. Gen. Omar Al Bashir and backed by the Nationalist Islamic Front of Hassan Al Turabi. The conflict has acquired an international dimension: the Sudanese government is providing support for Islamist groups in neighboring countries; Ethiopia, Eritrea, and Uganda have responded by backing the insurgents in the Sudanese People's Liberation Army (SPLA); and the Sudanese government, in turn, has extended its support even to non-Islamist opponents of its neighbors, including the Lord Resistance Army in Uganda. In 1994, in an unprecedented move, Ethiopia, Eritrea, and Uganda formalized their support for the Sudanese opposition, with Eritrea becoming the host for the National Democratic Alliance, a coalition of northern and southern Sudanese groups.

Connected to the politics of the Sudan and the Horn on one side, Uganda is also linked to the conflict in Rwanda between the Tutsi Rwandan Patriotic Army and the Hutu forces. The RPA organized and trained in Uganda, recruiting its members among the Rwandan refugees there. Furthermore, the leaders of the RPA, including Paul Kagame, received their early military and political training fighting alongside Museveni in the National Resistance Army. When the RPA came to power in Rwanda, Uganda emerged as its most important backer. This has made Uganda an enemy for the Interahamwe, which in turn carried out incursions in western Uganda.

The conflict in Rwanda spilled over directly into Zaire, as refugees and *génocidaires* streamed across the border and were settled in enormous camps. Eastern Zaire, already weakly controlled by the faraway government in Kinshasa, turned into a hotbed of armed groups and criss-crossing conflicts. In the

107

refugee camps, the Interahamwe and the remnants of the FAR regrouped and rearmed. The Tutsi minority groups in eastern Zaire, whom the government sought to expel, organized and armed as well. A smattering of smaller groups, such as the MaiMai, fought their own battles for obscure causes, changing alliances whenever it suited them. Opponents of the regime in Uganda also found eastern Zaire a convenient refuge. Out of the chaos emerged the alliance of Zairian Tutsis, other opponents of Mobutu, the new RPM government in Rwanda, and Uganda that consolidated in the AFDL, leading eventually to Kabila's victory. All of the above participants have a direct stake in the area. Eritrea and Ethiopia do not, but their political link to Uganda and Rwanda led them to support the AFDL as well.

As the AFDL advanced deeper into Zaire toward Kinshasa, Angola was also pulled into the conflict. Mobutu was a supporter of Jonas Savimbi's UNITA (*União Nacional para a Indepêndencia Total de Angola*), the armed movement that has fought the Angolan government since independence in 1975. This gave Savimbi an incentive to support Mobutu—and the MPLA government a good reason to contribute to his downfall. The MPLA as a result sent some military units and, above all, ferried back into Angola the Katangese gendarmes and their descendants, protagonists in old Zairian conflicts who had been living as refugees in Angola since the 1960s. UNITA also provided some troops in a vain attempt to prop up Mobutu.

A few months after the fall of Mobutu, the chain extended one more link to the Congo (Brazzaville): when fighting broke out during an election campaign between the supporters of President Pascal Lissouba and those of his rival, former president Denis Sassou-Nguesso, members of the old Mobutu army, the Habyarimana army, and the Interahamwe showed up fighting alongside Lissouba's troops, while Angola sent troops to help Sassou-Nguesso occupy the port of Pointe Noire, which Lissouba had allowed to be used to transship arms to Savimbi.

The most recent extension of the chain involves countries of the Southern Africa Development Community (SADC) as far south as Zimbabwe and Namibia. In summer 1998, history repeated itself in the DRC, as President Kabila faced an insurgency backed by Rwanda and Uganda very similar to the one that brought him to power some fifteen months earlier. Behind the formation of the new movement was the same combination of factors that led to Kabila's rise: lack of control or of a viable policy of reconciliation by the government in Kinshasa, fear of repression by the Congolese Tutsis, fear of incursions from the Congo by Uganda and Rwanda, and whatever political agenda the rebels may have added to the mix. The insurgency by Kabila was accepted, if not supported, by other countries in the region. It was clear to all governments that the demise of Mobutu was imminent in any case because his health was failing, and that there was no advantage in trying to keep him in power. The countries that were directly interested in Mobutu's downfall supported Kabila, and the rest acquiesced tacitly. But Kabila is not a dying man. He is an incumbent head of state threatened by an armed insurrection. Furthermore, the DRC is now a member of SADC. The solidarity among incumbent leaders that has been a constant in African politics has again come into play, with old leaders rallying behind Kabila, and new leaders rallying behind his opponents.

POLICIES WITHOUT RULES

All civil wars have repercussions beyond the country's borders as refugees flee, armed movements seek safe havens, and neighboring countries come under great pressure to take sides. But the long chain stretching across Africa shows that more is involved than a series of simple attempts by governments to protect themselves from the spillover of other people's conflicts onto their territory. Ethiopia and Eritrea did not have to get involved in Zaire to protect themselves, for example. The foreign policies of the new leaders are not simply based on the necessity to safeguard their countries, although this is of course the central preoccupation; rather, they also reveal a will to rebuild the entire region as they are rebuilding their countries, and to devise solutions for old conflicts, reconfiguring governments and forging new alliances in the process. A new bloc appeared to be emerging in the area until the fallout between Ethiopia and Eritrea in May 1998.

At the heart of this emerging bloc are the four leaders here discussed. While they have not agreed completely on all issues,

109

they have often acted in concert, showing a similar willingness to get involved in conflicts that do not affect them directly. This is the most unusual aspect of this emerging bloc—and one that separates the new leaders from others also involved in the chain of crises.

The conflict in Zaire in 1996-97 provides the clearest example. Rwanda and Uganda were directly affected by events in eastern Zaire and thus had a good reason to intervene. As the fighting spread to the entire country, and in particular to Shaba, Angola also had a direct reason to become involved, because the defeat of Mobutu would weaken Savimbi and thus improve the position of the MPLA government. But Eritrea and Ethiopia also supported Kabila's AFDL, with the Eritreans in particular providing technical support although they had no direct security or other interests at stake in Zaire. Rather, intervention was the result of a political choice to oust a government that symbolized the old Africa. African states have not manifested such commitment to an abstract notion in their foreign policies since their support for decolonization and for the ANC's struggle against apartheid. Even in those cases, the support was diplomatic and to some extent financial rather than military. African states did not commit troops to fight white regimes in other countries.

The new leaders' interventionism might have become a positive change in Africa had it been regulated by recognized principles. But the interventionism of the new leaders appears to be guided by expediency and solidarity with one another, not by principles. The prevailing reciprocal acceptance of each other by African leaders no matter what is happening in their countries has become virtually a law of silence among members of a mafia, and such *omertà* does not encourage governments to act more responsibly. However, the interventionism of the new leaders does not offer a better alternative.

The two major targets of the new leaders have been Omar Al Bashir and Mobutu Sese Seko—both indefensible characters with no legitimacy in the eyes of the international community and little in the eyes of their countrymen. Mobutu had lost most domestic support a long time ago—the ease with which Kabila's weak AFDL marched across Zaire was a clear indication that Zairians were not interested in keeping Mobutu in power. With the end of the Cold War, even former external supporters saw no reason to defend a leader whose only virtue was his pro-Western orientation and whose regime had itself become a source of instability rather than a bulwark against it. The Bashir government, which the United States placed on the international terrorist list, was feared by all its neighbors as a supporter of Islamist organizations; at home, it was resented by the non-Moslem population because of its imposition on all citizens of the *shari'a*, the harsh Islamic law, and opposed by many Moslems as well. Both the Sudanese and Zairian regimes were massive violators of human rights; even slavery, never fully extinct in the region, was on the increase in the Sudan. There was little regret when Mobutu was deposed, and there would be little if Bashir met with the same fate.

But what do the new leaders want in their place? The only indications are provided by the Democratic Republic of the Congo, and they are not reassuring. The choice of Kabila to replace Mobutu appeared guided by expediency. He had no legitimacy in Zaire, where he was virtually unknown in 1996; nor did he appear to have a particular vision for his country. There are reasons to believe that even his allies recognized the choice of Kabila as problematic from the beginning—it was months, for example, before he was recognized as the leader of the AFDL rather than simply as its spokesman. Like other governments that puzzled over the dilemma of where to find a credible successor to Mobutu, the new leaders most likely had few choices. For the DRC, they probably would have preferred someone akin to themselves: a capable, energetic leader, bent on economic reform, with a vision of how to stabilize the country, but with no interest in rushing toward electoral democracy—in other words, a more competent Kabila. When Kabila failed, the new leaders turned elsewhere.

To attain their goals, the new leaders did not hesitate to resort to force in the Sudan and in the DRC (twice in the latter country)—as they have done in their domestic struggles. In other situations, however, they have resorted to more diplomatic means, seeking to promote negotiations and to facilitate compromise. Ethiopia has attempted to mediate the conflict in Somalia, bringing together faction leaders for endless (and to date unsuccessful) rounds of talks. Eritrea, Ethiopia, and

111

Uganda have been major players in the efforts of IGAD to negotiate a solution to the Sudanese conflict. Uganda, Rwanda, and
Ethiopia are important participants in the summits on Burundi
organized under the auspices of the OAU. Thus what sets the
new leaders apart is not their rejection of diplomatic and political
solutions, but their willingness to resort to force when these fail.

What the new leaders have not envisaged, however, is political transitions brought about through democratic elections—the
solution favored by the international donors. In part, this rejection of transition through elections is the result of the same
beliefs that have caused them to reject multi-party democracy at
home. In part, it is also a realistic assessment of the situation;
neither Mobutu nor Bashir would allow themselves to be voted
out of power, and elections are not conceivable as a means of
state reconstruction in Somalia, or of ethnic reconciliation in
Rwanda or Burundi.

The interventionism of the new leaders is not the cause of
instability in the region, but a reaction to it. It remains nevertheless a worrisome trend. While it is an understandable
response to the failure of the United Nations and the international community to intervene constructively to correct glaring
problems, this interventionism falls outside all rules. It opens the
way for dangerous abuses, as demonstrated by the human rights
violations that occurred in eastern Zaire during Kabila's march
and continue in the Democratic Republic of the Congo.
Moreover, the new leaders' assertiveness can also turn into
aggression, as it did in the 1998 border conflict between
Ethiopia and Eritrea that risks destroying everything the two
governments have accomplished since 1991.

The Issue of Human Rights

When the refugee camps in eastern Zaire were broken up by the
AFDL and its Rwandan supporters in October 1996, the majority of the residents returned to Rwanda. An unknown number,
estimated to be between 200,000 and 300,000, headed deeper
into Zaire instead. How many of them were bona fide refugees
and how many were members of the Interahamwe and the former FAR is not known, but there were undoubtedly large numbers of women and children among them. International human-

itarian organizations lost track of these refugees for extended periods of time. After the fall of Kisangani in February, refugees started reappearing in that area, and some were eventually also repatriated. At the same time, reports also surfaced that many of the refugees had been systematically killed by soldiers, prompting speculation that this might have been the result of official Rwandan government or AFDL policy. Kabila was barely in power in Kinshasa when international human rights organizations, and eventually the United Nations, started calling for a full-scale investigation of the killings and for the punishment of the perpetrators. The U.N. investigation never took place. After reluctantly accepting the investigation in principle, the new DRC government stalled at every step of the attempted implementation. When U.N. investigators finally started their field work, they ran into local opposition—most probably ordered from above. In April 1998, the United Nations finally decided to recall the investigators. In the meantime, unofficial investigations by human rights organizations have uncovered evidence that killing on a large scale did take place, although no overall reliable assessment of the numbers has been provided.

In the absence of a complete investigation, it is impossible to reach conclusions as to whether the killings were the result of a deliberate decision by Kabila, of orders issued to the Rwandan soldiers by their government, or of actions by commanders in the field seeking revenge for the killings in Rwanda. But while it is unwarranted to accuse specific leaders for what happened, the episode is also a reminder of the abuses to which interventionism without principles and accountability could lead.

The Conflict Between Ethiopia and Eritrea

Assertiveness also entails the danger of aggression, particularly when two equally assertive leaders fall out with each other, as Meles and Isaias did in May 1998. This threatens to lead to a conflict nobody expected and apparently nobody wants, but from which the two governments appear unable to extricate themselves because compromise is not a part of political culture of either side. What makes this conflict particularly disturbing is that it does not involve vital interests for either side. It is thus much more difficult to explain than Rwandan and Ugandan intervention in the DRC.

The separation of Eritrea from Ethiopia after 1991 has proceeded smoothly, more so in fact than anyone dared to hope.
Despite the complaints of the Amhara Greater Ethiopia nationalists, most Ethiopians by 1991 accepted the inevitability of the
separation. Eritreans, for their part, voted overwhelmingly for
independence. Tensions that inevitably arose from time to time
over the details of separating the two countries were usually
solved fairly quickly. And while parts of the border were not
clearly demarcated, this was considered a problem that did not
need to be settled urgently.

In 1998, however, economic issues increased the tension
between the two countries. First, Eritrea decided to mint its own
currency, but it reacted badly when Ethiopia decided that, since
neither its own currency nor that of Eritrea was convertible,
cross-border trade between the two countries should take place
in hard currency. A further problem arose when the Ethiopian
government concluded that the fuel it imported from the
Eritrean refinery in Assab was overpriced, and that it could
obtain cheaper supplies from other sources. The decision left
Eritrea with a serious problem, since the Assab refinery originally had been built to serve Addis Ababa and the southern part of
Ethiopia and could not survive without the Ethiopian market.
There were no indications, however, that these tensions could
lead to war between such close allies.

Suddenly, in May, clashes occurred between border patrols
in the Badme area, an arid stretch of land of no particular economic importance. In a matter of days, both sides sent rein-
forcements, and in early June the two countries bombed each
other's territory. Many organizations and countries have been
trying to mediate the conflict since—above all IGAD, the OAU,
the United States, and Rwanda—but without results.

The main obstacle to a solution is not the intrinsic value to
either side of the area under dispute, but the style of the two governments: equally assertive, equally willing to resort to force,
equally driven not by international rules and principles but by
their own. These were precisely the characteristics that drove the
TPLF and the EPLF to fight and to win the war against
Mengistu, and that pushed the two countries to support Kabila
a long way from their borders. And when two movements used
to playing by their own rules and following their own principles

turn against each other, compromise is likely to be difficult and the possibility of prolonged conflict real. The progress both have made in the reconstruction of the state and the relaunching of economic activity is threatened.

AFRICAN SOLUTIONS FOR AFRICAN PROBLEMS

The interventionism of the new leaders is an attempt to work out African solutions for African problems—although one that itself causes major problems. "African solutions for African problems" has become a frequent call by the international community unwilling to supply the financial and manpower resources to provide international solutions to African problems. As normally used, "African solutions for African problems" is a rather vague call for Africans to take more responsibility, and a more concrete one for them to contribute manpower for peace-keeping operations—relieving the international community of a burden it is increasingly unwilling to shoulder. It is definitely not a call for Africans to develop different principles for dealing with conflict in their midst. The African solutions are expected to fall within the norms established by international organizations and the major powers. The African Crisis Response Initiative pro-posed by the United States—with the training of African troops to participate in internationally sanctioned peacekeeping opera-tions—represents such an interpretation of African solutions for African problems.

The interventionism of the new leaders represents another interpretation of the concept, one that goes well beyond African participation in internationally sanctioned interventions. It includes the idea that African countries will decide for them-selves how and when to intervene, whether or not such steps are sanctioned by the international community and fit international norms. It is also the interventionism of poor countries that face urgent problems with small military and financial resources but cannot afford not to act. The refugee camps in eastern Zaire were a problem Rwanda could not ignore. The ideal solution to the problem was to separate the refugees from the *génocidaires* and from the armed Hutus, to provide the former with the option to return to Rwanda or remain in camps, and to bring the *génocidaires* to justice and to disarm the militias. But such an

115

ideal solution was also a rich country's or a rich organization's solution—requiring ample financial resources as well as troops to carry it out. In the event, even rich countries and organizations found the undertaking politically and financially too costly and chose not to act. The poor countries had to do something, since they were threatened. Their solution was to attack the camps and force everybody out, dealing with the problem cheaply and effectively, but in violation of human rights and of international norms on refugees.

There is a parallel between the foreign policies of the new leaders and their policies at home. In both cases, they are attempting to provide solutions to intractable problems, and to do so despite the lack of financial, organizational, and manpower resources. The solutions are rough and ready, leaving much to be desired in terms of principles and norms. But they are solutions that can be implemented even by countries with few resources, while international principles often provide guidelines that can only be followed by organizations with abundant resources that African countries do not have and that the international community is not willing to make available.

Chapter 8

LOOKING AHEAD

I t was clear from the outset of this study that Uganda, Ethiopia, and Eritrea are not democratic. Closer analysis has further confirmed that all three governments continue to value control and directed change more than participation, although they are following a model of political and economic transformation that is markedly different from what African countries have pursued in the past. This model is not, however, one of democratic transition, at least not at this point. Indeed, a democratic transition is not conceivable in countries like these— countries that still have not solved the problems of power and authority and thus are not stable, de facto states that could become democratic.

The countries are not mired in static, authoritarian systems. There is a lot of ferment, with new structures of power and authority beginning to take shape. And at least in Uganda and Ethiopia, a dynamic process is under way that is beginning to create a degree of pluralism. The process is particularly strong in Uganda. If current trends continue, the countries may eventually evolve toward democracy, but by following an unorthodox path. As for Eritrea, at the time of this writing, it is difficult to see any signs of pluralism emerging. In the case of the first two countries, it is possible to envisage a scenario of incremental change eventually leading to democracy, as long as the governments succeed in maintaining stability and strengthening their capacity to make and implement policy; in the case of Eritrea, it seems more probable that a sharp break with the status quo will have to occur before such incremental change can become possible. Thus the difference is not simply one of time, but of process.

Even in Uganda and Ethiopia, however, it is by no means inevitable that the situation will continue to evolve in a direction favorable to democracy. The possibility of reversals exists, particularly as Uganda becomes more deeply enmeshed in domestic and external conflict and the threat of full-scale war between Ethiopia and Eritrea persists.

It is worth briefly reviewing here the common features in the process of transformation of the three countries and the peculiarities of each country's experience before turning to the issue of whether and how donors can increase the probability of a democratic transformation.

COMMONALITIES: TRANSFORMATION FROM THE TOP AND THE CREATION OF POLITICAL SPACE

The starting point for all three countries is a political tradition of transformation from the top through state power. This is the tradition of post-independence Africa, enhanced in the three countries by the fact that the governments came to power through military means.

The tendency toward top-down control is accentuated further by the weakness of economic and social structures. Peasant economies do not usually generate centers of economic power that can counterbalance the power of the state, although peasants as individuals are often adept at evading government control. The small modern sector in all three countries is either government-controlled or seriously decayed—or both. Social structures have also been badly disrupted by war and, in Ethiopia, by the attempts at forced collectivization and resettlement of peasants during the Mengistu period. In all three countries, government control thus remains strong less because of the state's overwhelming reach than because there are few countervailing centers of power.

The process of reconstruction therefore has been undertaken largely from the center and driven more by considerations of power and authority, as discussed earlier, than by those of democracy and participation. Whatever the initial intention of the leadership, however, the process of state consolidation has started redistributing power away from the military and in general away from the center. By strengthening the administration and promoting local government, the leaders have not only consolidated their own position but also encouraged the growth of more centers of power. Not all such centers are autonomous, or could resist reimposition of centralized control if the government so decided, but state reconstruction has contributed to a more pluralistic power distribution.

Economic liberalization has also resulted in some redistribution of power away from the government. Again, it is a slow process, hampered by the fact that these remain predominantly peasant economies and that the modern sector is quite small. The change is nevertheless significant, particularly in Ethiopia, where the urban elite was previously almost completely dependent on the government for its livelihood. The fact that civil servants can leave government service and make a better living for themselves in the private sector—and that bright university graduates are shunning public sector employment in favor of the business world—is seen by many Ethiopians as a significant political change.

Some new centers of power have also started emerging in that nebulous realm called civil society. Most visible is the growth of urban NGOs in Uganda and, slowly, the beginning of a similar process in Ethiopia. It is also probable, although extremely difficult to document without extensive research, that as rural areas settle down after the war, old and new community-based organizations will play a more important role. Personnel of some international NGOs working in rural areas in Uganda, for example, claim they have witnessed a flourishing of such organizations.

A process of state consolidation that started from the top down, by military movements with an authoritarian if not outright totalitarian tradition, has thus resulted in a degree of deconcentration of power—not just in the form of strengthened local or regional governments but also in the emergence of centers of economic and social activity independent of the government. Such deconcentration of power is not democracy. But it has, nevertheless, created conditions somewhat more conducive to democracy than those which existed before.

The one area in which little or no change has taken place, despite state reconstruction and economic liberalization, is the realm of competitive party politics. In the case of Eritrea, it is not necessary to probe deeply to explain the absence of change: the EPLF's hold over the country is so extensive, the leadership of

119

the party so monolithic, and its tradition of command and control so deeply rooted that there is no space for the formation of
independent parties. In the case of Uganda and Ethiopia, the
answer is not so obvious. In Uganda, there is space for party
activities. Despite the limitations discussed earlier, members of
opposition organizations sit in the parliament, and the mass
media (government and independent alike) report on the activities of the parties, their opinions on the burning issues of the
day, and the statements of their leaders. In Ethiopia, where elections have been formally competitive, the parties are numerous,
although the potentially most important ones are by no means
free to operate and are subject to much harassment. In both
countries, however, the parties appear as ambivalent about their
own role as the government is uncertain about how much space
to allow them. They advocate democracy on the one hand, berat-
ing the government for violating fundamental liberties, but they
also boycott elections, threaten violence, and often talk the language of liberation movements rather than of political parties,
making the government even more suspicious. While much
change is taking place in other areas, party politics remains
caught in a vicious circle. The implications will be discussed further below.

DIFFERENCES: POLITICAL STRATEGIES AND THE LOGIC OF ECONOMIC TRANSFORMATION

Although the process of state reconstruction controlled from
the top is increasing pluralism in Uganda and Ethiopia,
democracy is not the inevitable outcome. But the change taking
place points to the fact that maintaining a tightly controlled,
monolithic system is going to be extraordinarily difficult—
although Eritrea still appears able to do so a few years after the
end of the war. Just administering a country more effectively in
a decentralized manner promotes a degree of what could be
called spontaneous pluralism. Although it is insufficient to create democracy, the limited pluralism that is the unintended con-
sequence of the reorganization of state administration and the
revival of the economy is nevertheless a step in the right direction.

Uganda and Ethiopia differ not only in the degree of pluralism that is emerging, but also in its source—the political and

civil society sector in Uganda, and the economic sector in Ethiopia. In Uganda, increased pluralism in the late 1990s appears driven above all by politics. The NGOs are very active, and many are following, consciously, a reformist, incrementalist strategy of pressing for change on specific issues—for example, inheritance laws affecting women, or prison reform—rather than mounting a direct attack on the government to force it immediately to respect democratic principles. Pluralism is also developing within the NRM, with a growing number of "movementists" becoming convinced that the country must not only shift to multi-partyism but also do so sooner rather than later. Pluralism, in other words, is based on the existence of autonomous political actors, set on influencing the government's agenda, and sufficiently confident to accept short-term compromises on the road to long-term transformation. However, these independent political actors are few, largely urban, and in general do not represent mobilized constituencies. It is premature to equate such pluralism with democracy.

In Ethiopia, the situation is rather different. The NGO sector is still extremely weak—even the most enthusiastic participants talk about it as embryonic. The sector is a mixture of mostly international NGOs traditionally engaged in humanitarian relief and, to a much lesser extent, development work; weak indigenous NGOs still trying to define their role; and a few highly vocal and highly partisan organizations that appear more interested in lambasting the government on principle than in achieving results on any particular issue. The government, furthermore, remains highly distrustful of the NGOs, which it considers to be disguised opposition groups unless they can prove otherwise. The registration of a new NGO is a long, cumbersome process that easily takes over a year and often is unsuccessful.

Economic organizations such as the chamber of commerce are also regarded with suspicion by the government—less because they are seen as potential opposition parties than because they are seen as representatives of special interests, lobbying for policies that favor narrow groups. It is in some respects the same attitude that makes the government suspicious of NGOs: the government alone is the guardian of the public good, and it should not listen to organizations representing special interests. But the government cannot dismiss the demands of

121

business organizations and the private sector completely; having adopted an economic strategy based on market principles, albeit those of a "governed market," the Ethiopian leadership needs the private sector to grow and prosper and thus cannot completely ignore its demands. The NGOs, however, do not offer anything the government needs—not yet at least—and are more easily ignored.

The internal dynamic of the ruling party is also different in Ethiopia. Like the NRM, the EPRDF has its own internal divisions, not only among the member parties, but also within each of them. Tensions within the TPLF are particularly rife. However, while in Uganda the existence of different positions on key issues within the NRM—above all the transition to multipartyism—is freely discussed, in Ethiopia it is shrouded in secrecy, inevitably giving rise to wild rumors and conspiratorial interpretations.

What explains the difference between Uganda and Ethiopia? To some extent, it may simply be a matter of time—the transformation of Uganda has been under way since 1986, that of Ethiopia only since 1991. Ugandan NGOs have had more time to establish themselves, to develop strategies, and to learn to be effective than those in Ethiopia. To some extent, the difference may also be one of political culture, particularly of the culture of the political organizations. The TPLF has a much longer history than the NRM, a much more structured apparatus, and a tradition (rooted in its Marxist-Leninist background) of ideological unity achieved through much discussion but then strictly followed—not traits conducive to the acceptance of pluralism. The NRM wants to be an inclusive big tent, without a strong ideological line. Finally, it is also possible that differences in the leadership outside the government sector also play a part: the NGO sector possibly has attracted more capable leadership in Uganda than in Ethiopia—people more nimble at influencing the government without making it feel threatened.

PROBLEMS OF TRANSITION

The experiences of the three countries raise a host of questions about political, and possibly democratic, transitions. Three deserve special attention: the intricacies of pluralism, the issue of leadership, and the tension between the politics of principles and the politics of process.

The Intricacies of Pluralism

One question relates to pluralism, and specifically to the way in which different forms of pluralism come into play in democratic transitions. Democratic societies are pluralistic in a great number of ways. There is the pluralism of groups directly competing for the power to make decisions: political parties. There is the pluralism of interest groups seeking to influence decisions: the vast array of organized groups, lobbies, NGOs, professional associations, labor unions, business associations, and others, each pursuing its own narrower or broader goals. This pluralism is particularly pronounced in a market economy, which not only underpins a multiplicity of interest groups seeking to influence political decisions, but also frees the educated urban class from dependence on government service, increasing its political space. There is the pluralism of government institutions, both horizontal (brought about by the classic separation of powers and the existence of autonomous agencies of restraint) and vertical (the multiple layers of government that exist in a decentralized system). Finally, there is the pluralism of what Robert Putnam calls "social capital": the pluralism of the everyday, seemingly trivial associational life that develops when people are neither constrained by a totalitarian state nor hemmed in by a tradition-bound society.

We know little about how different forms of pluralism relate to the emergence of democracy, and in particular whether certain forms of pluralism must exist before others can also develop. The orthodox transition model assumes that all are important: democracy requires political parties, of course, but it also requires a vibrant civil society, which means an array of NGOs and community-based organizations, professional associations, and economic interest groups; in a rather vague manner, the supply of more diffuse social capital is also considered to be important to a democratic transition.

The experience of the three countries suggests that political parties are the weakest link in the development of pluralism. NGOs, business and labor groups, and community-based organizations arise fairly readily, unless the government forcibly closes all political space, as it does in Eritrea. Such groups can emerge even in what can be considered a fairly hostile environment, as in Ethiopia—particularly if they concentrate initially on goals that are not antagonistic but complementary to the government's, so that their gains can also be presented by the government as its own accomplishments. If foreign investment in improved telecommunications and power supplies, or increased availability of microcredit to peasant women, results in increased economic growth, this is a victory that can be claimed not only by the specific interest groups that advocated the change or undertook the project, but by the government as well. In Uganda, Museveni and the NRM can gain popularity with half the electorate by accepting the reforms pushed forward by women's groups—indeed, this may be the reason why women's NGOs are emerging among the most successful organizations in many countries.

By definition, however, the pluralism of political parties creates antagonism rather then complementarity. Governments are thus most suspicious of political parties and tend to give them the least political space. The opposition parties in turn attribute their own weaknesses to government treachery. The pluralism of political parties is thus the most difficult, contentious form of pluralism, and the slowest to get accepted. Yet the orthodox transition model nevertheless assumes that a pluralistic political process must start with the political parties so that multi-party elections can be held as soon as possible.

In addition to the inherent difficulty they face as organizations that must be antagonistic to the party in power, opposition political parties are also likely to suffer—as Uganda and Ethiopia show—because of their own histories and legacies. NGOs are a new type of organization in most countries, formed from the beginning with the expectation that they will function in a democratic system, or at least in a relatively open one, together with a great number and variety of other organizations. But the political parties expected to compete democratically at present often originated in non-democratic systems and are likely to bring to politics a non-democratic tradition very similar to that of the ruling party.

The pluralism created by NGOs, economic interest groups, and community-based organizations, as well as by the strengthening and decentralizing of government institutions, is not sufficient to make a political system democratic; that requires political party competition in an election process. Furthermore, such organizations are often weak and ineffectual, generating the illusion of pluralism without its substance—for example, when donors support many NGOs that are virtually clones of each other and do not represent distinct mobilized constituencies. But if the emergence of parties (both in government and in the opposition) capable of operating in a democratic system is the most difficult step in the development of pluralism, a democratization model that starts with party competition in elections, instead of ending there, must be called into question.

The Issue of Leadership

One of the conclusions of this study is that Uganda and Ethiopia are countries where democracy may emerge from the present situation through a reformist, incrementalist process, while in Eritrea a sharp break would probably be needed to start an evolution toward democracy. Does the difference reside in the quality of the leadership—simplistically, are Museveni and Meles "new leaders" while Isaias is not—or is the difference explained by underlying structural conditions? More generally, what is the role of leadership in a democratic transition?

An examination of the three countries suggests that leadership is crucial, although certainly not the only factor. It is not necessarily the leadership of one individual—particularly in the case of Ethiopia; one needs to consider not just Meles, but the top echelons of the TPLF. And it is not just leadership in the government, but in all other sectors of the society: officials at lower levels of government, leaders of NGOs, economic organizations, political parties. A democratic transition requires a new generation of leaders in all areas, not just in government.

The conclusion that leadership is crucial in the evolution of these systems is to a large extent obvious, since political systems in transition are by definition not institutionalized. Nor can such systems be expected to become institutionalized rapidly, since institutionalization is a matter of making an innovation a routine, and that takes time. Thus to say that leadership is all-important in these countries is to state that these are systems in transition.

125

Although leadership is crucial in all areas, Museveni, Isaias, and Meles together with the TPLF core are still the key to the changes taking place in their countries. They have provided a vision of how their countries should change, and they have shown themselves ready to innovate, seeking ways to address the old problems with new solutions. This does not mean that other solutions would not have been possible, or that other policies would not have brought about better results—better is in any case a matter of opinion. It only means that they made a conscious effort to devise new strategies to overcome old problems. This puts these leaders in a different category from most of today's African leaders, for whom power is an end in itself rather than a means to transform the country.

Dynamic leadership is a major asset in all three countries, but it is also the greatest threat to the consolidation of democratic systems, indeed of any system in the future. Two issues in particular need to be raised: one can simply be called the temptations of power; the other is the uneven development of leadership across the political spectrum.

It is not necessary to elaborate at length on the temptations of power. The problem is not just one of greed (though that often plays a role), but also that, the more important the role of a leader has been at a crucial moment of transition, the more reasons that person has to worry about relinquishing power. The problem is most evident in Uganda and Eritrea. Museveni's supporters and foes alike worry that if he were to disappear suddenly, he would leave behind a vacuum because institutions remain weak; they also worry that institutions will remain weak if he continues in power. In the case of Eritrea, the situation appears even worse, because Isaias dominates the EPLF as the EPLF dominates the country. In Ethiopia, Meles's power appears less personal because he is more subject to the collective control of the TPLF leadership. But that situation is also an obstacle to evolution toward a more democratic system, because it makes the party, rather than the elected officials, the center of power. In other words, none of the three countries appears close to solving the problem of moving successfully from a leadership-dominated to an institution-dominated system. All three are caught in the vicious circle where leadership remains crucial to further development but also prevents the consolidation of institutions that would safeguard the progress made as a result of innovative leadership.

The conundrum of leadership versus institutions does not affect just the government, but all organizations. Most organizations, including political parties, remain dominated by one or a few people—indeed, some consist of just a few people. It is impossible to estimate how many of the existing NGOs would disappear with their founders, or how many newspapers would fold if the editor gave up, but it would probably be a high proportion.

Finally, there is the problem of the uneven development of leadership. New leadership has emerged at the higher echelons of the executive, and it is beginning to emerge in a broader array of government institutions: in the regions in Ethiopia, in the independent agencies such as the Inspector-General's Office in Uganda, and, slowly, in the parliaments. New leadership is also emerging in the NGO sector and in economic institutions—both in organizations representing economic interest groups and, perhaps more important, in private sector enterprises. In Uganda at least, it is emerging in the mass media; even the government papers have learned to be more open, to provide more information, and to discuss controversial issues. All these are growing sectors with considerable dynamism. As pointed out previously, little new leadership has surfaced in the parties. Even where new leadership is emerging, it is still only a thin layer superimposed on sluggish organizations that have not caught the spirit of change. In all sectors, furthermore, dynamic new groups coexist with others that still appear quite static.

The Politics of Principles and the Politics of Process

Democratic systems are based on a set of absolute principles—above all, that citizens have inalienable rights and that a country must be governed by law rather than by the arbitrary decisions of individuals in positions of power. What makes democratic systems function in day-to-day practice, however, is not absolute principles, but a process of decision making that is based on bargaining and compromise. If democratic systems can function at all, it is because most fights are not over principles, but over negotiable issues, and because political actors are willing to accept half-measures and ad hoc solutions. The politics of high principles, on the other hand, easily creates intolerance rather than democracy: utopian systems tend to be totalitarian. Yet, without respect for basic principles, a political system ceases to be democratic.

In a process of democratization, the contradictory nature of democracy as a system governed by absolute principles but functioning in practice through deals and compromise is evident. Democratization can only succeed if all political actors, on the side of government and on the side of the opposition, accept the principles, but at the same time learn to play the not-so-noble game of democratic politics. The examples of Uganda and Ethiopia suggest three conclusions. First, the acceptance of democratic principles is a slow and difficult process, not only for the incumbent government, but also for opposition parties and other organizations that arise from the same historical experiences and political culture. The same parties that invoke democracy when they are in the opposition often do not live by democratic principles in their own organizations—especially when they come to power. Second, accepting the uncertainty and the compromises of the politics of process is as difficult for all political actors as accepting to abide by democratic principles. Third, the cause of democracy is not always advanced most effectively by those who focus on absolute principles; at times, it is the politics of process, with all its shortcomings, that moves democratization forward. The difficulty for domestic actors as well as for donors is to distinguish between situations that call for the politics of principles and those that call for the politics of process— in other words, to distinguish between what is desirable and what is possible.

Uganda, Ethiopia, and even Eritrea formally made considerable progress toward accepting democratic principles when they rewrote their constitutions. The most notable departure, in documents that otherwise appear unexceptional, is the recognition of the "movement" system as well as the multi-party system by the Ugandan constitution. The value of the constitutional provisions is limited in practice by three factors: some of the laws regulating the exercise of constitutionally recognized rights are restrictive, with press laws and laws regulating the registration of political parties and NGOs being the most controversial; the weakness of independent organizations makes it easier for the government to pass restrictive laws; and the extremist, non-democratic positions some of these organizations take lend some legitimacy to government repression in the eyes of many citizens. When political parties threaten violence, or when the independent press indulges in publishing libelous stories that cannot possibly be true, they make it easier for the government to maintain restrictive laws and encourage citizens to believe that democracy is a dangerous political system that could plunge their country into violence. The weak commitment to democratic principles by government and opposition alike creates a vicious circle.

But government and opposition groups also have difficulty accepting the democratic process. The politics of process appears to be gaining acceptance most clearly in Uganda, to a lesser extent in Ethiopia, and not at all in Eritrea. In Uganda, some NGOs have deliberately chosen the politics of process over the politics of principles. The opposition political parties, however, are rejecting process and insisting on high principles, as seen in their declared intention to boycott the referendum on multi-partyism. In Ethiopia, no organization appears to be articulating self-consciously a strategy based on process rather than principles, although some of the economic organizations appear to be doing so in practice.

The interplay between the politics of principles and the politics of process is a crucial issue in a process of democratic transformation that does not receive sufficient attention. For understandable reasons, analyses of democratization favor principles: a country is deemed to be on its way to democracy when it accepts a set of basic democratic principles formally and respects them in practice. Thus, democratization projects are designed to help countries strengthen the governmental and non-governmental institutions that embody the principles and ensure that they will be respected.

But how does a country develop a system based on high principles? Historically, the answer is: not quickly, not evenly across the board, and not without a great deal of pressure and resistance. Intellectuals committed to democracy may spell out the principles eloquently and nobly, but implementation is through politics, which is rarely noble. Organizations demand-

129

ing that a government suddenly convert to democracy, calling on the international community to impose sanctions if it does not, or threatening violence if all else fails, may be less successful in bringing about change than those setting more modest goals and pursuing them through the sometimes unprincipled politics of process. But the politics of process does not necessarily lead to democracy, even in the long run. It may lead simply to accommodation among members of a small elite, or to the co-optation of the opposition into the government, causing the process of transformation to grind to a halt.

There are no simple or, above all, general answers to the issue of when the cause of democracy is more likely to be moved forward by insistence on principles and when by acceptance of the slowness and imperfections of the politics of process. Each situation is different. In Uganda, there is sufficient pressure on the government from within and without to suggest that it is a time for process rather than absolute principles, and that the NGOs and the more liberal members of the NRM are advancing democracy more successfully than the more principled parties. In Ethiopia, the political space that allows organizations to work for incremental change is narrower and less promising, and the organizations capable of and willing to take advantage of opportunities to make modest gains are weaker. In Eritrea, finally, both the political space in which the politics of process might unfold and the organizations to play that game are lacking—as are organizations strong enough to confront the government on principles and to achieve results. Whatever transformation takes place in Eritrea in the short run must come from the top.

PROMOTING DEMOCRACY: THE LONG VIEW

The model of transition to democracy favored by donors—a short period of liberalization, followed by elections and by a long period of democratic consolidation through the strengthening of institutions of government and organizations of civil society—has little relevance for the countries under discussion. It assumes as a starting point a stable country, where the government has sufficient power to control the territory and where that power has already been institutionalized and thus transformed to a large extent into authority. It also assumes that, once the heavy hand of government is lifted, an underlying pluralistic society will be revealed, with well-defined interest groups that can organize themselves into political parties ready to compete for elections and with organizations of civil society ready to put pressure on the government. It is a model inspired by studies of the final stages of the democratic transitions in Latin America and Southern Europe, with their consolidated bureaucratic states and complex economies, but it applies poorly to Uganda, Ethiopia, and Eritrea—or to the numerous countries, above all but not exclusively in Africa, where the existence of the state is more fiction than reality, the government has little or no capacity to implement policy, and the economy has ground to a halt. The Democratic Republic of the Congo, Cambodia, or Bosnia are cases in point.

In such countries, the process has to start not with liberalization, but with state reconstruction, and state reconstruction can only be undertaken from the top. The alternative to such a top-down process is not a reconstruction of the state from below, an idealized coming together through a democratic process of highly participatory local communities. Realistically, the alternative to reconstruction from the top is Somalia: a breakdown of the state and infighting among factions until somebody manages to come out on top. Power and authority need to be generated before they can be decentralized and democratized. This means that foreign donors promoting democracy need to support governments in their attempts to reconstruct the state as much as they support organizations of civil society or the independent media in their efforts to promote participation.

In its dealings with the new leaders, the United States has followed an extremely ambiguous and ultimately unproductive policy. Relations with the new leaders have been close, and democracy promotion has played little part in the so-called partnership. Almost no pressure to adopt a more democratic stance has been put on the Eritrean government—by far the most autocratic and monolithic of the three. Ethiopia's fictitious election process has not received strong support, but it has not been strongly condemned either, and after some initial attempts to work with organizations of civil society and political parties, assistance in that country has concentrated on economic development. In Uganda, USAID has placed greater emphasis on

131

democracy promotion—supporting NGOs and seeking to strengthen parliament, for example, but pressure on Museveni to open the system to multi-party competition has been erratic.

The policy, however, has not been based on the acknowledgment that these countries cannot become instantly democratic and that they have to follow a different process. Rather, it has been built on the fiction that these are relatively democratic governments, which they are not. The conflict between Eritrea and Ethiopia and the second intervention by Uganda and Rwanda in the Democratic Republic of the Congo during 1998 have shattered this fiction of democracy, causing the new leaders to fall from grace and skepticism to mount about their intentions and their democratic commitment. In reality, these crises are not a deviation by the new leaders from the policies that have won them acclaim, but the downside of the policy of seeking stability and building the state that they have been pursuing all along.

Missing from the policy toward the new leaders is a serious debate about what can be done to help countries that start from a situation of state collapse to both address their immediate problems and move toward democracy in the long run. The dominant paradigm calls for immediate transition to democracy through elections and immediate conversion of the economies through the liberalization of their markets—which is not possible. Democracy is not going to emerge automatically from the efforts to rebuild the state or the economy, or even from a modest opening of political space. Donors need to continue pressing for democratization. But what is a realistic approach to democratization?

Some preliminary answers to this question can be found by revisiting some lessons learned from efforts to support economic restructuring, the other major structural transformation that donors have now been promoting around the world for almost two decades. Economic restructuring in Africa has been a slow and painful process, hampered by the same underlying conditions that make political change difficult. Several lessons emerging from this experience have relevance for political restructuring as well—in particular the importance of policy dialogue; the need to sequence reforms correctly, lest they do more harm than good; and the necessity of taking a long view of the process, accepting the inevitability of pain and conflict in the short run, and seeking ways to alleviate the problems.

The importance of policy dialogue is the most important lesson. Reforms imposed by the donors are not as likely to be successful as those negotiated between the donors and the recipients. Negotiations help donors understand better the problems faced by a country, leading to plans for change that are more realistic and more likely to be implemented. A similar policy dialogue needs to take place whenever donors seek ways to promote democracy. Each country is different; each situation entails different challenges and pitfalls; and policy dialogue would help in the development of realistic approaches to political reform. Through such a dialogue, donors can put pressure on governments to take steps to broaden political participation, but they can also learn more clearly what dangers such steps entail and what can be done to avoid them. In the end, the balance between what is desirable and what is possible can only be achieved through such a dialogue. If dialogue is not possible, it is pointless to seek to promote democracy.

The experience of economic restructuring programs has also shown that the sequencing of reforms is very important—it does matter which steps are taken first and which are postponed, and premature reforms can do more harm than good. The same is undoubtedly true for political reform, but we are far from understanding clearly what can work when. Elections, for example, can be a crucial step toward democracy, or they can be a setback, as they were in Ethiopia. There are situations where the cause of democracy may be better advanced by promoting decentralization, or a government of national unity, or even some forms of corporate representation than by insisting on elections. Crucial to the problem of sequencing is learning to understand when the problems of power and authority have to receive the most attention, and when the problem of participation becomes paramount. Much more needs to be understood about the sequencing of political reform measures.

No one expects an economic restructuring program to work quickly and painlessly. On the contrary, it is accepted that economic restructuring is extremely difficult in the early stages, and that it always creates hardship and often conflict—through higher unemployment and price increases, for example. Over the years, something has been learned about the typical problems created by economic reforms and about the corrective measures that can be put in place to alleviate the problems somewhat. The political restructuring involved in a transition to democracy likewise should not be expected to be smooth and painless. Much more needs to be learned about the crises and conflicts to be expected as a country seeks to restructure politically and about what can be done to reduce their negative impact. It is not realistic, for example, to interpret the emergence of conflict as a sign that a country is not becoming more democratic. This does not mean, of course, that conflict is always a good thing, or that all conflicts are a sign of progress toward democracy. It does mean, however, that it is not realistic to expect progress toward democracy without conflict.

An important aspect of any democratic transition is the emergence of new leadership. It is doubtful that donors can do much here: they can help train technocrats, and in fact are doing so, but leadership is a more complex phenomenon than technical competence. A real democratic transition probably cannot take place in a country until a new generation of leaders has emerged—with generation in this case understood not in terms of age but in terms of political outlook. In Ethiopia, Eritrea, and Uganda, such a generational change has started taking place with a set of leaders who have perceived the need for a new approach to the problems of their countries. They have brought about much change, but they may yet fail—particularly if they allow their countries to sink again into the quagmire of escalating armed conflicts. But the ranks of the new generation remain thin, and many more members are needed in government ministries, among parliamentarians, in the judiciary, in local government, in the political parties and organizations of civil society, and in the private sector. In demographic terms, a generation is reckoned at about thirty years. The emergence of a new political generation may well require a similar time span.

ABOUT THE AUTHOR

Marina Ottaway is a Senior Associate and Co-Director of the Democracy Project at the Carnegie Endowment for International Peace. She is also Adjunct Professor of African Studies at the Nitze School of Advanced International Studies, Johns Hopkins University. She has carried out research in Africa for many years and has taught at the University of Addis Ababa, the University of Zambia, the American University in Cairo, and the University of the Witwatersrand in South Africa. She has written extensively on the political evolution of Southern Africa and the Horn.

Most recently, Dr. Ottaway has been working on problems of democratic transformation in Africa: *Democracy and Ethnic Nationalism: African and Eastern European Experiences* (Overseas Development Council, 1994) is a study of problems of democratization in multi-ethnic societies; an edited volume, *Democracy in Africa: The Hard Road Ahead* (Lynne Rienner, 1997), discusses obstacles to democratization on the continent. She has also just completed a study of elections in post-conflict society for the U.S. Agency for International Development.

ABOUT THE CARNEGIE ENDOWMENT

The Carnegie Endowment for International Peace was established in 1910 in Washington, D.C., with a gift from Andrew Carnegie. As a tax-exempt non-profit organization, the Endowment conducts programs of research, discussion, publication, and education in international affairs and U.S. foreign policy. The Endowment publishes the quarterly magazine, *Foreign Policy*.

Carnegie's senior associates—whose backgrounds include government, journalism, law, academia, and public affairs—bring to their work substantial first-hand experience in foreign policy. Through writing, public and media appearances, study groups, and conferences, Carnegie associates seek to invigorate and extend both expert and public discussion on a wide range of international issues, including worldwide migration, nuclear non-proliferation, regional conflicts, multilateralism, democracy-building, and the use of force. The Endowment also engages in and encourages projects designed to foster innovative contributions in international affairs.

In 1993, the Carnegie Endowment committed its resources to the establishment of a public policy research center in Moscow designed to promote intellectual collaboration among scholars and specialists in the United States, Russia, and other post-Soviet states. Together with the Endowment's associates in Washington, the center's staff of Russian and American specialists conduct programs on a broad range of major policy issues ranging from economic reform to civil-military relations. The Carnegie Moscow Center holds seminars, workshops, and study groups at which international participants from academia, government, journalism, the private sector, and non-governmental institutions gather to exchange views. It also provides a forum for prominent international figures to present their views to informed Moscow audiences. Associates of the center also host seminars in Kiev, Ukraine, on an equally broad set of topics.

The Endowment normally does not take institutional positions on public policy issues. It supports its activities primarily from its own resources, supplemented by non-governmental, philanthropic grants.

138